FINANCIAL TIMES
STYLE GUIDE

FINANCIAL TIMES
STYLE GUIDE

Compiled by Colin Inman

Cartoons by Roger Beale

FINANCIAL TIMES

PITMAN PUBLISHING

PITMAN PUBLISHING
128 Long Acre, London WC2E 9AN

A Division of Longman Group Limited

First published in Great Britain 1994

© The Financial Times 1994

British Library Cataloguing in Publication Data
A CIP catalogue record for this book can be obtained from the British Library.

ISBN 0 273 60568 2

1 3 5 7 9 10 8 6 4 2

Photoset by PanTek Arts Ltd,
Maidstone, Kent.

Printed and bound by Bell and Bain Ltd., Glasgow

*The Publishers' policy is to use paper manufactured
from sustainable forests.*

ACKNOWLEDGEMENTS

This book is a distillation of Financial Times practice built up over many years. Richard Lambert and Max Wilkinson read the whole manuscript and made many amendments. Peter Martin revised and added to the Financial Glossary and updated the stock market indices guide. Geoff Jones wrote the original FT style book, published five years ago. His co-author was Wolf Luetkens, former foreign news editor and leader writer, who continued to provide valuable comments on style up to his death in 1992. Debbie Hargreaves checked and improved the energy glossary. Clive Cookson prepared the nuclear glossary. Michael Donne, former aerospace correspondent, provided the basis of the section on aircraft names. Advice on the spelling of foreign names was given by Victor Mallet, Alex Nicoll, David Dodwell, Angus Foster, Chrystia Freeland, Bob del Quiaro, Stephen Fidler and Leyla Boulton. Jancis Robinson and Nick Lander gave advice on the food and drink entries. Adrian Dicks provided the stock market indices guide. Paul Davies of Oswald Hickson wrote the section on law and libel. Ray Hughes, former legal eagle, wrote the entry on courts. Andrew Jack provided details on accountants. Other colleagues too numerous to mention offered pungent critism, tomfool comments and wise advice, not necessarily in that order.

CONTENTS

INTRODUCTION

"He [Boot]'s supposed "to have a particularly high-class style: 'Feather-footed through the plashy fen passes the questing vole'....would that be it?" "Yes," said the Managing Editor. "That must be good style."

(Evelyn Waugh, *Scoop*, 1938)

"My spelling is Wobbly. It's good spelling but it Wobbles, and the letters get in the wrong places."

(A.A. Milne, *Winnie-the-Pooh*, 1926)

"Journalism – an ability to meet the challenge of filling the space."

(Rebecca West, New York Herald Tribune, 1956)

"Literature is the art of writing something that will be read twice; journalism what will be read once."

(Cyril Connolly, *Enemies of Promise*, 1938)

"Try to preserve an author's style if he is an author and has a style. Try to make dialogue sound like talk, not writing."

(Wolcott Gibbs quoted by James Thurber, *The Years with Ross*, 1959)

The Financial Times, reputation rests on the accuracy of the information in its pages, the depth of its reporting, the perception of its analysis and the clarity of its writing.

Accurate use of language is vital in maintaining the paper's quality. Consistency through the various sections of the newspaper is also essential to secure and retain a busy reader's confidence.

Style is not a burnish applied after an article has been written. Stylish prose requires precision in observation, in note-taking, in analysis, in composing sentences and in the use of words. Clarity of thought is the key to clarity in writing.

This book sets some guidelines for good practice and outlines some rules that should be followed. It highlights recurring errors, gives advice on writing and includes lists of preferred spellings. A reference section contains glossaries of financial, scientific and technical terms.

The FT's readers are alert to factual errors in the paper. They are also alert to the misuse of the English language, misspellings and incorrect grammar. In one sample month readers castigated the FT for:

referring to *the* former Yugoslavia and *the* Ukraine
calling the Irish pound the punt
writing *though* instead of *although*
misspelling *espresso* and *salutary*
using a plural verb after the word *none*
using the indicative mood after *if*
starting sentences with *but* and *and*
writing *in tandem* when *in parallel* was meant
using the present participle of verbs in captions
writing *like* instead of *such as*
using (unqualified) the phrase *ethnic cleansing*
writing *hamstrung* instead of *hamstringed*
using foreign words where equivalent English ones were available
referring to British soldiers in Northern Ireland when no others were
   involved
writing *apologium* as if it were the singular of *apologia*
writing *per capita* where *per caput* would have been more accurate
using unnecessarily long words such as *inarticulateness* and
   denouncement
referring to the Canadian prime minister as a *premier*.

Not all of these complaints passed unchallenged.

Anyone writing news stories should try to keep a few basic rules in mind:

1. Try to answer the questions of who, what, where, why, when, how and how much within the first three paragraphs of a story.

2. Make every word count. Use short simple sentences and short words rather than long ones. Make one striking point in the opening sentence of a story, ideally using 14–20 words, not more than 25. Prefer the active voice to the passive, the transitive verb to the intransitive.

3. Prefer the full stop to other forms of punctuation. Use **and** and **but** sparingly at the start of sentences and, especially, paragraphs.

4. Keep paragraphs, particularly the first, to no more than about 40 words. Avoid using the same opening word in successive paragraphs.. Remember Fowler's contention that the paragraph is a unit of thought not of length.

5. Write in the language of everyday speech, not that of politicians, lawyers or trade unionists. Prefer English words to foreign ones unless no accurate equivalent exists. Explain anything the readers may not understand.

6. Do not let your own opinions invade a news story. Do not tell the reader what to do or think.

7. Explain early in the story the function of the organisation/s you are writing about. The writer should do this; the sub should not have to.

8. Keep abstract nouns to a minimum (**situation, condition, problem**) and consider whether words such as **really, however, for instance** are needed. Do not ascribe eyesight to months (**next month should see an improvement in the figures**...). Such vaguely metaphorical terms can always be avoided. Give words a precise meaning.

9. Be accurate in the use of quoted matter, especially in headlines.

10. Remember what part of the paper you are writing for. Phrases and abbreviations that are acceptable in the financial and markets sections may need fuller explanation in the news and features pages.

11. Do not pepper your copy with too many acronyms; they are a visual distraction and are often unnecessary.

12. Remember that two-fifths of FT readers live outside the UK. Therefore avoid the words **we** and **here** when referring to the UK. Also avoid being too UK-specific with the seasons of the year and points of the compass.

13. Bear in mind the possibility of libel and send a story to the lawyers if you think there is any risk.

English is a living and changing language, and FT writing will always react to this. This guide should be regarded only as reflecting the newspaper's practice in mid-1994. New words and new meanings for words emerge, principally from the US. They should be considered carefully before acceptance and explained where necessary. **A slew of new results** may be a familiar phrase to readers in the US, but not (yet) to those in Britain including the bulk of the FT's readership.

All FT journalists, as anyone else, are encouraged to consult *Fowler's Modern English Usage* (as revised by Sir Ernest Gowers; a new revision by Robert Burchfield is in preparation). Gowers' *The Complete Plain Words* is also recommended, as are books on language by Philip Howard. *Waterhouse on Newspaper Style* by Keith Waterhouse can also be commended, especially to anyone who is thinking of moving to a tabloid newspaper.

Hard copy subbing: how it never was

A final word to subeditors: one result of the paperless office, where all editing is carried out on small rectangular screens, is that it is all too easy to force stories into a sort of uniformity of style, removing any individuality and elegance they might have possessed. Good writing should be recognised – and left as it is.

ALPHABETICAL
LISTINGS

A

a and **an** Write **an** before a word starting with **h** only if the **h** is silent. Thus: **a hero, a historic, a hostage, a horse, a hospital, a hotel, an heir, an honest, an honour, an hour, an honorary.**

For other words, it is governed largely by ease of pronunciation before the initial letter (either consonant or vowel), such as: **a eulogy, a European, a ewe, an FA cup match, a one, an Opec, an £8m profit, a unanimous, a Unesco, a union, a university, a useful.**

A-bomb Write atomic bomb except in heads.

Aachen is a city in Germany.

Aargau is a canton of Switzerland.

abattoir is a slaughterhouse and has one **b** and two **t's.**

abbreviations, acronyms and contractions Several hundred abbreviations are used in every issue of the FT. In a few instances the abbreviated form is so well known that there is no need to spell it out first: **BBC, CIA, EU, FBI, MP, Nato.** In most other cases write the words in full on their first appearance.

Put the abbreviated form in parentheses after the name *only* if the organisation is little known or if the letters of the abbreviation are not in the same order as the full (often translated) name: **the German Social Democratic party (SPD).** Elsewhere the abbreviated form can be used at next mention: **The Organisation for Economic Co-operation and Development said in its annual report.... The OECD added that...** Too many parenthesised abbreviations break the flow of copy.

Try to avoid too many abbreviations in a story: **the Union** can be used instead of **the EU; the agency** for **the IEA,** etc.

If the abbreviation is pronounced as a word it is written in upper and lower case: **Aids, Daf, Nato, Gatt, Unicef.** The definite article is not normally needed. Where the abbreviation is pronounced as the individual letters it remains in capitals: **the BBC, ICI, the OECD.** The definite article is sometimes needed.

The only exceptions to the above rules are for units of measurement, where internationally agreed standard forms are used: **kg, km/h, kWh, lb, mph**. Also **ie** and **eg**.

All abbreviations use letters only with no points between them and are closed up to figures: **10am, 20ha, 30kWh, 40mph, 50kg, 60BC**; where there are two abbreviations they are separated: **10m b/d**.

Plurals generally just append a lower case **s**: **MPs, SDRs, the 1980s**.

See also **Abbreviations**, pages 139–148; **Organisations**, pages 200–211; **Unions**, pages 225–226.

Aberystwyth is a town in Dyfed, Wales.

Abidjan is the capital of Côte d'Ivoire.

aboriginal, **aborigines** refer to indigenous populations. Native Australians are **Aborigines**.

abridgment is preferred to abridgement.

absorption, with a **p**, is the process of **absorbing** something; **absorbtion** is not a word.

accents A number of accents are available on the FT system and should be used where appropriate: the acute **é**, grave **è**, circumflex **â**, cedilla **ç**, Umlaut or diaeresis **ä**, the tilde **ã**, and the dotless **i**, which in Spanish carries an acute accent (**í**) and in Turkish no accent; the Scandinavian **ø** and a number of other accents are not available on the FT system.

Accents are never used on capital letters.

Anglicised words Many words from other languages are now accepted as English. Where the accents make little or no difference to the pronunciation they can be omitted: **debacle, depot, elite, matinee, menage, precis, regime**.

Where the accents affect the pronunciation, they should be retained: **café, cliché, communiqué, soupçon**. If you use one accent on a word, use them all: **émigré(e), pâté, protégé(e), résumé**.

Common accented words:

Académie française	Elysée	Pöhl
Aérospatiale	française	Saint-Saëns
Béla Bartók	François	São Paulo
Bogotá	Freischütz	señor
Bohème	Générale	Sinn Féin
Bölkow	Götterdämmerung	société
Brontë	Kraków	théâtre
chargé d'affaires	Länder	Weizsäcker
Citroën	Medellín	Wörner
Dáil	Musée	Württemberg
Electricité	Pérez de Cuéllar	Zauberflöte

access is a noun but preferably not a verb; note the adjective **accessible**, with an **i**.

accommodation can often be replaced by houses, flats, lodgings; a common error is to spell **accommodate** with only one **m**.

accordingly Try **therefore** or **so**.

accountants can usually be referred to as, for example, **Coopers & Lybrand**, **the accountancy firm**, or **the accountants**. Some may try to push the label **management consultants** when referring to themselves; beware of this.

The principal accountancy firms are:

Name of firm	*Shortened form*
Coopers & Lybrand (Deloitte dropped)*	Coopers
KPMG Peat Marwick (McLintock dropped)	KPMG
Price Waterhouse	PW
Ernst & Young	E&Y
Touche Ross†	Touche
Arthur Andersen (with an e)	Andersen
Grant Thornton	
BDO Binder Hamlyn	BDO
Pannell Kerr Forster	PKF

*Coopers' insolvency arm is Cork Gully.

†In most countries Touche Ross merged with Deloittes, creating a firm called Deloitte Ross Tohmatsu (DRT) or a variation on that theme.

Auditors are not synonymous with accountants. Auditors have a statutory function to perform and since 1991 have had to be separately registered, inspected and regulated. All auditors are accountants, but far fewer accountants are auditors.

Note that insolvency practitioners are appointed individually not as a firm: so refer to **Mr Arthur Green, receiver to Brown and White** or **partners at Grey, Green, appointed receivers to**...

Receiverships or administrative receivership are handled by **receivers**; administrations are handled by **administrators**; liquidations are handled by **liquidators**.

Achilles heel A small but fatal weakness, and **Achilles tendon**, a fibrous cord connecting the calf muscles to the heelbone, are given apostrophes in some reference books but not in others; for simplicity we should omit the apostrophe. *Brewer's Dictionary of Phrase and Fable* elegantly avoids the issue by referring to the heel of Achilles.

acknowledgment is preferred to **acknowledgement**.

acronyms *see* **abbreviations**.

acts of parliament take initial capitals for their full titles: **the Finance Act**; where referred to generically use lower case. Titles of bills are always lower case.

AD comes before the figure it refers to and should only be used on dates before **AD1000**; **BC** comes after the figure: **50BC**.

addenda is the plural of **addendum**.

Adirondack Mountains are in New York State in the US.

admittedly is an overused word: **admittedly ICI's results were affected by a slack world market**. Who makes the admission? and why apologise? **However** may be a preferable word if one is needed. Note that **admissible** is often wrongly spelt as **admissable**.

adverbs There is no need for a hyphen between an adverb and the verb it qualifies: **a keenly contested election**; **a wholly owned subsidiary**; unless ambiguity would result: **a little used car** or **a little-used car**.

In news stories do not start a sentence with an adverb: **Realistically the target date**....Some relaxation may be permitted in features.

adviser, with an **e**, is someone who acts in an **advisory** capacity.

affinity is mutual: you can have an affinity **with** something or **between** things, but not **to** or **for** something.

aficionado, an ardent supporter, has only one **f**.

African-American is a term that is increasingly being applied to US blacks. It is not yet in general use in the UK.

African National Congress is South Africa's oldest political organisation. It was banned in 1960 and unbanned in 1990.

Afrikaners are white South Africans of Dutch or Huguenot descent who speak **Afrikaans**.

Afrikaner Weerstandsbewiging (AWB), the Afrikaner Resistance Movement, is an extremist rightwing organisation in South Africa founded by Eugene Terre Blanche.

age Hyphens should be used in phrases such as **the 75-year-old president**; commas in **Mr Albert Hall, 75, said**... But there is no need to to refer to someone's age unless you want to draw attention to his or her youth or longevity. Note the spelling of **ageing** (not **aging**).

agree Prefer **agree on, to** or **with** to just **agree**.

Aids is an abbreviation of **acquired immune deficiency syndrome**. It is a medical condition and diseases affecting people are **Aids-related diseases**. Sufferers are susceptible to bacteria and viruses that are harmless to healthy people. Aids is caused by a virus called **HIV** (human immune deficiency virus), which is usually spread by sexual contact, blood transfusion or contaminated injection needles.

air force is usually lower case: **the Ruritanian air force**; but capitals should be used for specific titles: **the Royal Air Force**.

Air Force One is the name of the US president's aircraft.

air force ranks *see* **military names**.

aircraft names There is an almost bewildering number of aircraft and aero-engine designations and a variety of ways of describing them.

Where possible abbreviate a manufacturer's name after initially spelling it out: **British Aerospace** first, then **BAe**; **General Electric of the US**, then **GE**; note that the British **General Electric Company (GEC)** has no connection with the US company.

Airbus Industrie can be abbreviated to **AI**, and **McDonnell Douglas** simply to **Douglas** when writing about commercial aircraft; when writing about military aircraft or for other purposes it must appear in full, and it must never be abbreviated to **McDonnell**.

Pratt & Whitney should only be abbreviated to **P&W**, and only then if unavoidable. Similarly, **Rolls-Royce** must never be abbreviated to **Rolls**, and **R-R** should be avoided if possible. The best solution is to refer only to **Rolls-Royce**.

When writing about aircraft, the word **plane** should never be used. The correct words are **aeroplane, aircraft** or **airliner;** where military aircraft are concerned **fighter, bomber, helicopter, combat aircraft**. Even **jetliner,** horrible though it may be, is preferable to plane. **Warplane** is occasionally permissible in headings where there is no space to write **military aircraft** and where neither **fighter** nor **bomber** are strictly accurate.

To achieve some uniformity when writing aircraft and engine designations, and to simplify a complex system, the FT broadly adopts the manufacturers' own principles: where an aircraft designation involves both basic initials (denoting the manufacturer's name) and a number, followed by a number indicating how many passengers the aircraft can carry, the two numbers are separated by a hyphen, as follows:

> **Airbus A300-600, A310-300, A319, A320-200, A330-600R, A340.**
>
> **British Aerospace BAe-111, BAe 125-800, BAe 1000, BAe Hawk 100, BAe Hawk 200, BAe RJ75, BAe RJ80, BAe RJ100.**
>
> **Boeing 737-500, 747-400, 757-200, 767-300, 777.**
>
> **Learjet 31A, 35A, 60.**
>
> **McDonnell Douglas DC-10, MD-11, MD-80, MD-87, MD-90.**

Thereafter the aircraft can be referred to as the **A320, 737, MD-11** or **747** etc, to save space. Only Boeing aircraft should be referred to by the number only. Only Airbuses have no hyphen between letter and number. The objective must always be clarity and accuracy, and if achieving this means spelling a designation out in full, we should do so.

Where an aircraft already has a name, it should be used, initially in conjunction with the manufacturer's own name, and thereafter by itself, for example in:

Beech Starship
British Aerospace Jetstream, Concorde, Harrier
Canadair Challenger
Panavia Tornado.

The **European Fighter Aircraft (EFA)** is usually called the Eurofighter and is built by a consortium with the same name. To avoid confusion, we describe the aircraft as the **EFA** or **Eurofighter**, and describe the company as the **Eurofighter group** or **consortium**.

When referring to aero-engines, the same rule applies, as in the **Rolls-Royce RB211**. Where there are various versions of an engine, the specific variant's number should always be included in the first instance, for example **RB211-524** or **RB211-524G** or **RB211-535**, but thereafter can be simply written as the **524** or **524G** or **535**. Note that some Rolls-Royce engines are named after rivers: the **RB211- Trent** can be called the **Trent** subsequently.

In some cases, engine designations are extraordinarily complex. For example, one of the most widely used engines is the **General Electric (US) CF6-80C2**. It should be written like that, with the hyphen falling between the basic type **(CF6)** and the variant number **(80C2)**.

When in doubt consult Jane's *All the World's Aircraft*.

airlift is a noun but preferably not a verb; prefer **flown to safety**.

airlines Names of airlines, especially US carriers, are often misspelt. Check with an expert if you are in doubt. Note that aircraft fly **to** or **from** an airport rather than **into** or **out** of it.

Note the following:

Aer Lingus
Aerolineas Argentinas
Air-India *hyphenated*
America West *two words*
American Airlines *parent company AMR*
Continental Airlines
Delta Air Lines *three words*
El Al (Israel Airlines)
Icelandair
KLM Royal Dutch Airlines

Northwest Airlines *Northwest one word, no capital W, parent company NWA Continental Airlines*
Southwest Airlines *Southwest one word, no capital W*
TWA (Trans World Airlines)
United Airlines *parent company UAL*
USAir *one word, first three letters capitalised*
Virgin Atlantic Airways.

airports **Heathrow Airport–London** and **Gatwick Airport–London** are official styles; **London's Heathrow airport** is less cumbersome.

Ajaccio is the capital of Corsica.

Albuquerque is a city in central New Mexico.

Aldeburgh is a town on the Suffolk coast.

algae is strictly the plural of **alga**, but alga is never referred to, being too small to bother about.

alibi is the fact of being somewhere else, not an excuse.

all right is preferred to **alright**.

All Souls College, Oxford, has no apostrophe.

allege Be very careful not to allege things yourself. Give the source of any allegation.

Note that a Mr Black who is in custody may have been arrested for **alleged corruption** or **on charges of corruption**. He is not, however, facing **charges of alleged corruption** since alleged corruption is not an offence.

allies is normally lower case: **the Gulf war allies**. Use a capital only when referring to the Allies of the UK during the second world war.

almanac has no **k**, except in the titles of some books.

alsatian is the dog, not **alsation**; note the lower case **a**.

alternative

"The notion that because it is derived from Latin alter (one or other of two) alternative cannot properly be used of a choice between more than two possibilities is a Fetish." (*Fowler's Modern English Usage.*)

Alternative can be used to mean a set (often a pair) of possibilities: **We have no alternative; if we refuse, what are the alternatives? Choice** can often be used as an alternative to **alternative**.

Alternate means taking turns.

altos is the plural of **alto**.

alumni is the plural of **alumnus**.

America's Cup, an international yachting trophy, has an apostrophe.

American Take care: it can refer to anyone from Canada to Cape Horn. FT style is to write US for the United States, not USA.

Americanisms Many Americanisms have wormed their way into English usage, and there is probably no way of getting rid of them again. Hundreds are now fixed in the language (**commuter, executive, freight, mail, radio, teenager, truck**), and many are improvements. The advance of others should be resisted. In the list below the British-English form is normally preferred to the American English.

Note that titles of American institutions adopt English spelling: **defence** not **defense; labour** not **labor**.

American	*British*
aluminum	aluminium
antenna	aerial
appeal	appeal against
attorney	lawyer
attorney	solicitor
automobile	car
check	bill
check	cheque
corporation	company
cut back	cut
fall	autumn
garbage	rubbish
gasoline	petrol
hike	rise
inventories	stocks
jewelry	jewellery
loan	lend
lose out	lose
meet with	meet
neighborhood	district
ouster	dismissal
outside of	outside
post *results etc*	report
protest	protest against
rent	hire
run	stand *for office*
slate *verb*	schedule
slew *noun*	lot, number, quantity
subway	underground
talk with	talk to
toward	towards
transportation	transport
vacation	holiday
visit with	visit

amid is preferred to **amidst**.

amoebae is the plural of **amoeba**.

amok, a state of murderous frenzy, is preferred to **amuck**.

among is preferred to **amongst**.

ampersands should be used where corporate bodies use them as part of their name; in abbreviations of company names; and in charts and tables to save space.
  Note particularly:

  Marks and Spencer is **M&S** at later references; note that the shops proclaim Marks & Spencer
  Cable and Wireless becomes **C&W** at later references
  American Telephone and Telegraph later references **AT&T**
  Pratt & Whitney later references **P&W**.
  R&D research and development
  S&L savings and loan.

anaesthetic is correct spelling; beware of the American **anesthetic**.

analogous means **like**; **analogue**, commonly used in audio and computer technology as the forerunner of **digital**, should not be spelt **analog**.

analysts Be as specific as possible: **financial analysts, industry analysts**.

Andalucia is a region of southern Spain.

Andhra Pradesh is an Indian state.

Anglo has an initial capital and is hyphenated if the word that follows is capitalised: **Anglo-Catholic, Anglo-Indian, Anglophile, Anglo-Saxon**.

annex is a verb meaning to attach to something larger; an **annexe** is something that has been annexed.

antennas is preferred to **antennae** as the plural of **antenna**.

anti as a prefix is unhyphenated unless the base word is capitalised, or a confusing concatenation of vowels would occur: **anti-aircraft, anti-American, antitrust**.

anticipate means to forestall not to expect. Someone who has anticipated marriage may well find herself expecting something.

Antwerp is a city in Belgium; the Belgian name is **Antwerpen**.

apartheid was the South African system of enforced racial segregation, established in 1948. It was formally abolished in 1991.

Apennines are mountains in Italy.

apexes is the plural of **apex**.

apologia is a singular noun; it comes from the Greek word απολογια not from Latin.

apostrophes The apostrophe (') is gradually disappearing. It is leaving **Earls Court**, though not yet **Regent's Park**; and as Philip Howard points out in his entertaining essay in *A Word in Time*, it has vanished from countless trade names **(Barclays Bank, Currys, Dillons, Mothers Pride, Diners Club)** and the titles of newspapers and magazines **(Farmers Weekly)**. More place names have joined the list, perhaps not least because it makes life easier for signwriters: **St Andrews**. The trend is likely to continue. When in doubt consult an atlas or gazetteer.

However, the apostrophe (') is still used: (*a*) to show the possessive case; (*b*) to show an omission; (*c*) in a few plurals; (*d*) in some Irish names.

(a) Possessives An additional **s** after the apostrophe is normally used if the word ends with an **s**. But be guided by pronunciation. If the extra **s** would not be sounded in speech do not add it: **Mr James's book, his boss's views** (one boss), **his bosses' views** (lots of bosses), **Siemens' results, for goodness' sake, John Lewis's sales, Barclays' profits, Dickens's novels**. Note also an **MP's** (singular); **MPs'** (plural).

It is possible to use the possessive of Lloyds Bank **(Lloyds')** but not of **Lloyd's** the insurance market.

The phrases **10 years' imprisonment, two weeks' holiday** can be regarded as descriptive genitives (with apostrophe) or adjectival phrases (without). We should retain the apostrophe: this conforms with the singular, where it is inevitable: **a year's imprisonment**.

Also note **Achilles heel** and **Achilles tendon**; and **Lord's**, the cricket ground.

Terms such as **futures market** are adjectival and need no apostrophe.

(b) Omissions in news stories and features always write **he is** not **he's**, **it is** not **it's**, **will not** not **won't**, except in direct quotes. In the less formal context of Weekend FT occasional relaxation of this rule may be permissible.

An apostrophe does not precede words such as **bus, cello** or **phone**.

(c) Plurals the apostrophe is not needed in words that do not have a logical plural such as **Boeing 757s, the 1980s, two MPs, six NCOs, 12 QCs**; nor in compound nouns such as the **Three Choirs Festival**. It is still needed with single letters: **dot the i's, cross the t's, the three R's**.

It can be omitted from plurals of words that are not normally nouns: **ifs and buts, whys and wherefores** (though one would not expect to see these phrases in the FT).

(d) Irish names **O'Fiaiach, O'Riordan** for example.

apparent It might be better to write **clear, plain** or **obvious**. *See also* **clear**.

appeal is intransitive, so people **appeal against a decision**, they do not just **appeal a decision**; but this American phrase is now used regrettably often in British-English.

appendices is the plural of appendix.

appoggiatura is a musical ornament; note the spelling.

appraise is to evaluate, estimate the worth of; **apprise** is to inform.

approximately Shorter words are **about** and **roughly**.

aquariums is the plural of **aquarium**.

Arab and Persian names It is impossible to transliterate precisely or consistently from Arabic into English all the time, partly because of accepted tradition **(Cairo, Damascus)** and partly because Arabs themselves have different ideas about how their names should be spelt in English.

Many family names and place names begin with **al- (the)**, as in **Hafez al-Assad** of Syria or **Saddam Hussein al-Takriti** of Iraq. Often the **al-** is omitted altogether as in **Riyadh, Kuwait** or **President Assad**. Normally use a small **a** in the **al** (except at the beginning of a sentence), followed by a hyphen and a capital letter for the name that follows.

Avoid the elided, spoken form often used in some journals (as in **Ar-Riyadh** or **Farouq ash-Sharaa**), and avoid also the confusing use of an apostrophe to represent a glottal stop **(Koran** not **Qu'ran)**. Local use in Egypt and francophone north Africa, however, compels us to write **el-Alamein** and **el-Oued**. We also write **Abdul-Amir al-Anbari** instead of **Abd al-Amir al-Anbari**.

Beware of titles like **Sheikh, Sayed** and **Ayatollah**. Mr Sheikh is like Mr Sir.

Some common names and words:

Yassir Arafat

Basra

Dhahran

Muammer Gadaffi

hajj

Jeddah

Koran

Moslem

al-Nahyan Ali Akbar Hashemi Rafsanjani *Mr Rafsanjani at second mention*

Saddam Hussein *Mr Saddam at second mention*

Farouq al-Sharaa

Shia *not* Shi' ite

Aran is an island off Donegal, north-west Ireland; **Aran Islands** are a group of three islands off Galway on the west coast of Ireland; **Arran** is an island off the south-west coast of Scotland, in the Firth of Clyde.

arbitrator weighs evidence from both sides in a dispute and hands down a judgment; a **mediator** listens to both sides and tries to bring them to an agreement.

archbishops *see* **churchmen**.

archipelagos is the plural of **archipelago**.

Argentines are people from Argentina (not **Argentinians**).

army is normally lower case: **the British army**.

army ranks *see* **military names**.

16

Arunachal Pradesh is a state in India.

as of write **on, after, since**.

Ashkenazim are German or east European Jews; **Sephardim** are Jews of Spanish or Portuguese descent.

Asunción is the capital of Paraguay.

auditors *see* **accountants**.

auger is a thing for boring holes; **augur** is to predict or presage.

autarchy is absolute sovereignty; **autarky** is self-sufficiency.

automata is the the plural of **automaton**.

average, mean, median, norm to obtain an **average** add the numbers and divide by the number of items; a **mean** is the midpoint between two extremes; a **median** is the middle number of points in a series; the **norm** is standard for a group.

avoid

Some words and phrases that have become overused. Avoid them in any but their true sense:

at this moment in time	finalise	influential *esp about*
beleaguered	giant	*periodicals*
boom	glitch	ironically
broker *verb*	gravy train	key
burgeon, burgeoning	green light	literally
catastrophic	guesstimate	magnate
circles	healthy *except bodies*	major
crisis	hike *except as a walk*	manic
cutbacks *cuts*	hopefully	massive
dramatic	huge	meaningful
escalate	in excess of	panic
perception	rocketed	spend *noun*
persons *people*	salami tactics	street fighter
player *except sports-*	schizophrenic	strike action *strike*
man or musician	sell off *sell*	tight-lipped

pressure *verb*   situation   track record *record*
pressurise   slash   unprecedented
prestigious   slump   unveil
prior to *before*   soar *markets*   upcoming
punter   reportedly   sources

See also **clichés**

Azerbaijanis are people from Azerbaijan; the word **Azeris** is often used as an abbreviation but should if possible be confined to headlines.

B

Ba'ath party Note the apostrophe.

bacilli is the plural of **bacillus**.

background Beware of writing background where you may mean **explanation, experience, history**, etc.

bacteria is the plural of **bacterium**.

Baddawi is a refugee camp in Lebanon.

Baden-Württemberg is a state in Germany.

Baghdad is the capital of Iraq.

Bahamians, not **Bahamans**, come from the Bahamas.

Bahrain is preferred to **Bahrein**.

bail, bale Detained people and boats are **bailed out**; parachutists **bale out** and companies are **baled out**. But the words are largely interchangeable.

balk, baulk The verb is to **balk**; but a **baulk** of timber.

balloted, with one **t**, is the past tense of the verb **ballot**.

Bar The **Bar**, meaning the legal profession, has a capital **B**.

Barbadians come from Barbados.

barbecue is preferred to **barbeque**.

baroque, as a style of architecture, music, etc, has a lower case **b**.

Barrow-in-Furness in Cumbria has hyphens.

basically is often used but rarely necessary.

Basle is a Swiss city and canton; this spelling is preferred to **Basel** or **Bâle**.

battalion has two **t**'s and one **l**.

BC appears after the figure, as in **55BC**.

Beaufort scale measures wind speed. It ranges from 0 (calm) to 12 (hurricane).

Force	Description	Force	Description
0	calm	7	moderate gale
1	light air	8	fresh gale or gale
2	light breeze	9	strong gale
3	gentle breeze	10	whole gale or storm
4	moderate breeze	11	storm or violent storm
5	fresh breeze	12	hurricane
6	strong breeze	13–17	(used in the US)

The scale was devised by Sir Francis Beaufort (1774–1857).

bedouin is a nomadic desert Arab; the plural is the same.

beg the question means to assume the truth of what you are trying to prove as part of the proof. The phrase is almost invariably used incorrectly to mean **raise the question**. Possibly the best example of beg the question is **Have you stopped beating your wife?** The example quoted in Brewer's *Dictionary of Phrase and Fable* is: "To say that parallel lines will never meet because they are parallel, is simply to assume as a fact the very thing you profess to prove."

Beijing, formerly spelt **Peking**, is the capital of the People's Republic of China.

Belarus, former Soviet republic, was more commonly known as **Belorussia** or **Byelorussia**.

Belém is a city in Brazil.

Benelux countries consist of Belgium, Netherlands and Luxembourg; strictly the economic union within the EU of these countries.

beneficent, meaning generous, is often misspelt.

benefit leads to **benefited** and **benefiting**, with one **t**.

Bern is a city and canton in Switzerland.

betting odds Write 2–1; 5–4 on. However, in a sentence such as **odds were quoted of 2–1 on Tony Blair becoming the next leader of the Labour party**, the **on** can cause confusion. Odds of **2–1 on** are really 1–2, ie, you place a bet of £2 and get back £1 plus the stake if you win. With odds of **2–1** (against), your £2 bet will recoup £4 plus the stake. It is therefore important to make the precise odds clear; in the example above it might appear that the betting on Mr Blair was 1–2 (on) rather than, as presumably intended, 2–1 (against).

between Write **between £5 and £6; between £5m and £6m; between 1926 and 1930; between 30,000 and 35,000** (not between 20 and 30,000).

Beverly Hills in California; note the spelling.

biannual means twice a year; **biennial** means once every two years. Both are best avoided to prevent confusion.

bias The FT should be free from bias, whether political, racial or sexual. This does not mean, of course, that the paper does not express judgments and opinions: leaders, features and bylined columns do so every day. But it is important that news stories are unbiased and that distortions are not introduced during editing.

The path to neutral copy is strewn with mines. In a number of subjects, especially those relating to sexual equality, no clear and acceptable solutions have yet been agreed. But we have to abide by some rules, and these are outlined below.

Note that no reference should be made to a person's age, colour or religion unless these are directly relevant to a story.

business It is true that **businessmen** is rarely precise and generally includes some **businesswomen**. However, to write **businessmen and businesswomen** is clumsy; **business persons** is inelegant; **business people** or the

21

business community are slightly better. Sometimes **people in business** will be found to be an acceptable variant; sometimes just **business** can be substituted. **Executives** is also a popular solution, **business managers** or just **managers** possibilities.

chairmen and chairwomen A man heading a committee is often a **chairman** and should be referred to as such; a woman heading a committee is sometimes a **chairwoman** and should be called a chairwoman, unless, of course, she calls herself a **chairman**. However, some organisations now elect a **chair** or even a **chairperson**. Do your best to avoid using these terms; this is sometimes achieved by writing: **Ms Grey, who chairs the council's finance committee**. Other possibilities are phrases such as **head of**...or **in the chair**.

colour Black people are **blacks** but **political correctness** *qv* means that black is being replaced by **Afro-Caribbean** (or even by **African-American**); white people are **whites**. When writing about what the South Africans (used to) call **coloureds** we should use quotes and include an explanation such as: **"coloured" (mixed race) population**.

defence spending is often used as a euphemism for **military spending**.

ethnic groups It is important not to write **immigrant community** when referring only to a group of people of the same ethnic background (members of the Pakistani community in Bradford, for instance); it is probable that they have been in Britain for generations; to call them immigrants is incorrect.

firemen can easily be replaced by **firefighters** or **fire crews**, which are in any case likely to be more accurate terms.

foremen may well be *supervisors*.

guerrillas, freedom-fighters and terrorists A freedom-fighter to one person is a terrorist to another. Care is needed. **Freedom-fighters** are usually self-described and the term should be avoided. **Guerrillas** is a safer and more neutral description for people who actively oppose an elected government, though it may confer a degree of approval. **Paramilitaries** is a neutral term that can be applied to both sides.

    Terrorist seems sometimes to have been reserved for stories about atrocities by the IRA; unless this term is used evenhandedly we may be accused of lacking objectivity: **unionist leaders' anger at the recent wave of terrorist killings in Northern Ireland yesterday overshadowed...** Here the word **terrorist** seems to have been reserved for the IRA. Remember that terrorist attacks by Unionist/Loyalist sympathisers also take place.

Killers and murderers are possible alternative terms.

An **execution** is the carrying out of a sentence of death passed by a court of law. Terrorists or guerrillas **kill, murder, shoot** or **assassinate** their victims; they do not execute them.

Unionist is preferred to **Loyalist** in stories about Northern Ireland.

he and she, his and hers Try to avoid writing **he** where the context could refer to either sex. This is often not easy: **he or she** as a simple replacement for **he** looks clumsy. Replacing **he or she** by **they** or **their** is often a solution, provided the rest of the sentence is adjusted to fit. Or rephrase the sentence to avoid using pronouns.

manhours, manshifts This is what may happen by slavishly obeying current dogma on sexual neutrality. The writer's version was: **Selby produced coal at an average of 7.5 tonnes a manshift in the past year, compared with an average of 4.7 for all British Coal deep mines. However, it should be able to produce coal at above 10 tonnes a manshift – and has done so in bursts. Late in July last year, Selby produced a record 9.03 tonnes a manshift.**

When this copy reached the revise sub, **manshift** had been changed to **shift**, thus suggesting that the total output of the mine was 9.03 tonnes in a shift – doubtless the lowest figure in British coalmining history.

This is nonsensical. **Manshift** and **manhour** should be regarded as having no connection with the word man. **Working shift** and **working hours** are possible alternatives but there is no objection to continuing to write **manshift** and **manhour** where necessary.

mankind is an old word referring to the human race; there is no justification for assuming that it refers only to men, and no need to replace it with a neologism such as **humankind**. But writing **humanity** or even just **people** may avoid giving offence.

policemen are **police or police officers**; pejorative terms should not be used.

religion Religious belief should not be mentioned unless it is of direct relevance to a story. This is often the case in stories about Northern Ireland and the Middle East, but rarely elsewhere.

spokesmen, spokeswomen are acceptable; **spokespersons** is not; try **official** or **representative**. Where companies are concerned there is often no need to refer to a person at all: **ICI said**...

women In general the FT calls women what they want to be called; many women, especially of advanced years, like to be referred to as **Mrs** rather than **Ms**.

Where marital status is not known **Ms** is used; some women prefer to be called Ms, and regard it as an infringement of personal liberty for inquiries to be made about their status.

Authoress, Jewess, poetess, wardress and probably **manageress** should be avoided. **Actress, horsewoman, waitress** are still commonly used.

There is no need to refer to the sex of **doctors, lawyers, nurses, professors** or **teachers** unless of direct relevance to a story and no need for a female form of **executor, painter, priest** or **usher**.

Remember that **mayoresses** and **ambassadresses** are the wives or escorts of **mayors** or **ambassadors**; a female mayor is a **mayor**.

In some industries asexual job descriptions have been devised: **station manager** for stationmaster.

biased has only one **s**.

bid is frequently and legitimately used in takeover stories; in other contexts it is liable to overuse.

bill A parliamentary bill is always lower case.

billion is **1,000 million**; abbreviation **bn**.

biological terms Plants and animals have two scientific names indicating the genus and species. This is the binomial system. These names should be printed in italics, the first word having an initial capital: *Daphne mezerium*, which may be abbreviated to *D. mezerium* in an article referring to a number of daphnes. When a generic name is used on its own it should be printed in roman type and lower case.

bishops *see* **churchmen**.

black **In the black** means in profit in the UK, but the opposite in some other countries.

black box is an aircraft's flight recording equipment, often used to determine the cause of accidents.

blobs An average issue of the FT contains 30–40 blobs or bullet points. They are acceptable to show an addition to a story, especially where the subject matter is not precisely that covered by the main story; and to itemise a number of examples so that the return to the main text can be easily found.
   In other instances think carefully about whether the blob has any useful function.

bloc is a group of people or countries sharing a common interest or aim; not **block**.

blueprint is often (wrongly) used in place of **plan** or **scheme**.

Boer, literally farmer. Boers are descendants of the Dutch or Huguenot colonists who settled in South Africa.

bogey, bogy, bogie A bogey or bogy is a mischievous spirit; it is also par for a hole in golf or one over par; a **bogie** or **bogy** is a small railway truck or a set of wheels at the end of a railway coach.

Bogotá is the capital of Colombia.

book titles should be printed in italics; newspaper and magazine titles in roman type. Quotation marks are not used.

boom is a grievously overused word; avoid it unless writing about people messing about in boats.

Bophuthatswana is a South African "independent" state set up under apartheid for the Tswana people.

borrowed should not be used as a passive verb. A heavily **borrowed** group is a heavily **indebted** group.

borstals are now **Young Offender Institutions**.

Bosnia-Hercegovina not **Herzegovina**.

Bosporus is the strait between European and Asian Turkey; this spelling is preferred to **Bosphorus**.

bottom line is acceptable if used precisely to mean the net profit shown at the bottom of a profit and loss account; but do not use it metaphorically to mean the outcome of a process or discussion.

bougainvillaea is easily misspelt.

brackets, parentheses and dashes Parentheses can be indicated in four ways: square brackets, round brackets (parentheses), dashes and commas.
    The main use of **square brackets** is for inserting clarifying words into a passage being quoted: **The chairman said: "The tariff increases [in France] have hurt our competitive position."** The words within the brackets are not part of the quoted text.
    Of the others **commas** should be used where the least interruption to the flow is intended; dashes and round brackets for greater interruptions.

Round brackets should be used sparingly as a signal to a hurried reader that the words are of secondary importance. When the end of the bracketed passage coincides with the end of a sentence observe the following rules: if the whole sentence or a sequence of sentences has been enclosed in brackets the stop precedes the bracket. **(That is all.)** If only part of a sentence is in brackets, the full stop follows. **That is all (at least for the time being)**.

The bracketed passage should not be so long that the reader, when she comes to the end of it, forgets where she was when it began.

Dashes are useful for inserting important additional information into a sentence, provided the flow of the sentence is not interrupted: **The Dutch, Belgians and Germans – but not the French – are taking part in the Nato exercise**. But not: **Dutch, Belgian and German troops – the French are not taking part – are on manoeuvres in the area**. Used singly, dashes can convey surprise or make a point, but avoid using dashes as (in Ernest Gowers' words) a "punctuation maid-of-all-work that saves him the trouble of choosing the right stop".

Brands Hatch in Kent has no apostrophe.

Brasília is the capital of Brazil.

Braunschweig, the German city, is preferred to the English spelling **Brunswick**.

Britain   Great Britain is England, Scotland and Wales; it is sufficient to write Britain; the UK is England, Scotland, Wales and Northern Ireland; the British Isles is the whole lot including Ireland. The Isle of Man and the Channel Islands are crown dependencies; they are part of the British Isles but not part of the UK.
British people are **Britons**.

broker is preferred to the American **brokerage**, except when referring to the operation rather than the individual or institution carrying it out. Be as specific as possible: **stockbroker**, **insurance broker**, **shipbroker** unless the context is absolutely clear.

Bruges, in Belgium, is preferred to the Flemish spelling **Brugge**.

budget is lower case except for the annual **Budget** presented by the British chancellor of the exchequer; **budgeted** has only one **t**.

buffaloes is the plural of **buffalo**.

bureaux is preferred to **bureaus**.

Burkina Faso, the West African republic, was formerly called **Upper Volta**.

Burma is still Burma, not **Myanmar** in the FT.

Burmese names U is a Burmese title equivalent to **Mr** and should be omitted. It is best to use the full name throughout. Women's names are a minefield and it is also best to spell them out in full.

bus, busing is the practice of moving schoolchildren by bus to achieve a social or racial blend; not **'bus, bussing**.

but, and Objection to the use of **but** and **and** to start sentences is described in Fowler as a lingering superstition. There is no objection to this practice provided it is kept in control.

bylaw, bypass, byproduct have no hyphens; **by-election** has one.

bylines In the International edition of the FT all bylines carry the place of origin, including stories from London. In the London paper stories written in Britain carry the writer's name only; others include the place of origin.

Where two or more writers are involved it is usual practice for their names to appear in alphabetical order; but informal agreement may vary this when a journalist called, say, Zylstra has done the bulk of the work. With a single column byline, attempt to place the name on the first line and the place – including the word **in** – on the second:

> **By Violet Green**
> **in Ouagadougou**

Avoid multiple bylines, especially in single column stories.

In feature bylines avoid giving more prominence to the interviewer than the interviewee. **John Major talks to Philip Stephens** is correct, not the other way round.

C

cabinet is lower case.

cacao is the tree from whose seeds cocoa and chocolate are made.

Caernarvon is a port and resort on the north Wales coast; but note the spelling of Lord Carnavon.

calendar is an almanac; **calender** is a machine used in papermaking.

calibre refers to the internal diameter of the barrel of a gun, not to weight. Usual measurements are in fractions of an inch **(.303 rifle)** or millimetres **(152mm howitzer)**. Note that the zero before a decimal point is dropped.

Cambodia is preferred to the official name **Kampuchea**.

Cameroon in West Africa became a German colony in 1884; was divided in 1919 into the **Cameroons**, administered by Britain, and **Cameroun**, administered by France; it became a republic in 1961, consisting of Cameroons and part of Cameroun. The rest of Cameroun joined Nigeria.

Canute knew his feet would get wet; his courtiers believed they would not.

canvass is to survey opinion, especially political opinion; canvas is a durable material for making sails, tents, etc.

CAP is the **Common Agricultural Policy** of the EU; note use of capitals.

capability is often used to mean **potential ability**, and care should be taken not to overuse it; **is capable of** probably means **can**.

Cape Town in South Africa is two words.

capital gains tax is lower case.

capitalise If you mean **profit by** then say so.

capitals The world of e.e. cummings is not yet here, but until it is, the FT believes that the fewer capital letters we use the better. Places and organisations begin with a capital; personal titles generally do not. When in doubt use lower case unless the result looks silly or is confusing.

acronyms FT house style is to use upper and lower case where the initials are pronounced as a word, **Nato**; retaining capitals where the letters are pronounced, **ICI**. *See also* **abbreviations**.

armed forces Use lower case if possible: **the British army, the Israeli air force**; but use capitals for specific names: **the Royal Air Force, the Luftwaffe**.

government and politics The word **government** should be in lower case whether a specific government or otherwise. Thus, the **Chinese government, western governments**. Note that **parliament** does not take a capital P except when referring to the **Houses of Parliament**. Also note **the administration** (in the US), **the cabinet, Labour party, the opposition, politburo, the press**.

A **Socialist** belongs to the **Socialist party**; **socialism** describes his belief. A **Communist** denotes attachment to the **Communist party**; lower case for **communism** or **communist propaganda**. A **Conservative** is presumably conservative, and a **Tory**. Note also **the Crown**.

In the US, members of the Republican party are **Republicans** (and may well be democrats); members of the Democratic party are **Democrats**, but usually also republicans; **senators** are members of the US **Senate; congressmen** are members of **Congress** or **House of Representatives**.

Political labels derived from proper nouns retain their capitals: **Gaullism, Jacobite, Keynesian, Luddite, Maronite, Marxist, Napoleonic, Thatcherite**.

A government **green/white paper** is lower case; parliamentary acts take initial capitals only for their official titles: the **Criminal Justice Act**; names of acts used generically **(environment act, finance act)** are lower case; so are names of bills.

The **Budget**, as presented annually by the UK chancellor of the exchequer, takes a capital; any other budget is lower case.

Also note the **civil service, civil servants, the left, leftwing, the right, rightwing**.

measures Most abbreviations of weights and measures are lower case: **lb, kg, b** (for barrel), **rpm, mpg, kph** and so forth. Other abbreviations follow internationally accepted usage: **Btu, kW, kWh, MW**. *See also* **measures**.

Note also **special drawing rights (SDRs), the Deutschemark** which should be referred to as the **D-Mark**.

organisations Normally organisations, ministries, etc, have initial capitals: **the Bank of England (the bank), Cambridge University, the central bank** (except the Irish **Central Bank**, which is its title), **Chancery Division** (of the High Court), **county court** (but **Surrey County Court**), **Court of Appeal** (not the **appeal court**), **Department of Trade and Industry, European Commission (the Commission), European Community (the Community, the Twelve), High Court, House of Commons/Lords (the house), House of Representatives, International Monetary Fund (the fund), Queen's Bench, Senate, Supreme Court, Treasury, World Bank (the bank)**.

When using an English translation of a foreign name, lower case should be used: **the German defence ministry; the Indonesian ministry of foreign affairs**.

Subcommittees and less permanent organisations are in lower case.

people When referring to specific office holders, the title is lower case: **Mr John Major, the British prime minister; Mr Thomas Bloggs, the Ruritarian minister of external affairs**. A capital should be used only as a personal title: **President Clinton**. But this will not occur often since you should write **Mr Clinton** on second and subsequent references.

There are a few exceptions to this rule such as **Black Rod, God, Lord Privy Seal, Master of the Rolls, the Queen, the Pope, the Speaker**, where to drop the capitals might lead to confusion. But note **chancellor of the exchequer, Treasury secretary**. *See also* **Names and titles**.

places Definite geographical places and regions take initial capitals: **Central America, the Gulf, the Highlands, the Middle East, the Midwest, North Carolina, North Pole, North/South Korea, North-West Territories, West Midlands**.

But descriptive terms are lower case: **western Europe; north Wales; the south-east, the north**. **West Germany** and **East Germany** are now **west Germany** and **east Germany** except when referring to the countries existing before reunification.

The **third world** is lower case, but should be avoided if possible. The **developing world** or **developing countries** are better descriptions.

religions **Christian** (noun and adjective) should be capitalised; also **Buddhist, Hindu, Jewish, Moslem, Protestant, Roman Catholic, Semitic, Shintoist,** but **the church, heaven, hell, mass, papal, pagan, satanic.** *See also* **churchmen.**

miscellaneous Lower case letters are used for Latin abbreviations such as **eg, ie,** though their use is discouraged.

Trade names must start with a capital letter: **Thermos, Hoover, Valium, Biro**; but the use of such trade names as generics should be avoided. *See also* **trade names.**

Names of newspapers and periodicals are set in roman type. Do not cap **the** unless it is part of the title: **The Times, the Financial Times.**

Historical periods take an initial capital: **the Depression, the Middle Ages, the Reformation, the Renaissance, the Restoration**; but write **baroque, renaissance** when referring to styles of music, architecture, etc.

Also note:

anglicise	labrador *dog*	siamese twins
arabic figures	Lent	Speaker, the
autumn	Lord Privy Seal	spring
bill *parliamentary*	Mafia *Italian*	Stone Age
(British) embassy	May Day	summer
Christmas day	the new year	Thanksgiving day
Easter	New Year's day/eve	transatlantic
first world war	panama *hat*	transpacific
french dressing	Pershing missile	turkish bath
french window	plaster of paris	U-boat
general election	portland stone	utopia
Good Friday	Queen's Speech	venetian blind
H-bomb	royal assent	winter
High Court	second world war	
the king	Semitic	

captions Try to use full names in captions but do not use titles: **Tony Blair at Blackpool yesterday: critical of government policy.**

Name people from left to right; make sure the caption names relate to the correct people.

Avoid being cryptic: **Brown: incandescent.**

cargoes is the plural of **cargo.**

Caribbean has one **r** and two **b's**,

carmaker is one word.

cartel, an alliance between businesses aimed at reducing or eliminating competition in a particular market. Cartels fix prices, limit available supplies and pool profits. In politics a cartel is an alliance of parties or interests to promote common aims. Business cartels are usually illegal.

case Fowler says that "there is perhaps no single word so freely resorted to as a trouble-saver and consequently responsible for so much flabby writing." **In the case of** can almost always be removed; as can other uses of the word **case**.

catalyst accelerates a chemical reaction without itself suffering any permanent change. It is more than just an agent.

catholic means universal; the church is **Roman Catholic**.

caviar not **caviare**.

ceasefire is one word.

ceiling is too often used to mean **maximum** or **limit**.

cello should be written without an apostrophe.

celsius, temperature scale, is the same as **centigrade**.

censure is to criticise severely; **censor** is to control or suppress the behaviour of others; a **censer** is a pan in which incense is burnt.

centred on, not **around**.

chairman, chairwoman *see* **bias**.

chamois is both singular and plural.

Champs-Elysées in Paris has a hyphen.

Channel tunnel, capital **C**, lower case **t**; do not abbreviate to Chunnel.

channelled has two **l's**.

chaos In a sample year's issues of the FT the word **chaos** appeared 441 times; possibly this is too many. **Confusion** or **disorder** may be preferred.

chaperon not **chaperone**.

charge is best used only as a transitive verb: **Mr Green was charged with fraud**; but he might also be **charged with alcohol**. It would be better to write **Mr Green was accused of fraud**. *See also* **allege**.

chateaux is the plural of **chateau**; the accent, as in the French original **château**, may be omitted.

cheap Goods are **cheap** or **expensive**; prices are **low** or **high**. Remember that cheap can be pejorative; **inexpensive** may be a better word.

Chequers is the UK prime minister's official country house in Buckinghamshire.

Chinese names In the Chinese-speaking world a name is usually made up of three characters, with the family name first (one character), followed by the personal name (two characters). In places such as Taiwan, Korea, Singapore and Malaysia the personal name is usually split in two: **Goh Chok Tong, Ho Chi Minh, Lee Hsien Loong, Lee Kuan Yew, Roh Tae Woo**.

Mr is now used with all Chinese names: thus **Mr Goh Chok Tong** becomes **Mr Goh** at subsequent references.

Many Chinese run together the second two names: **Mr Deng Xiaoping** followed by **Mr Deng**; **Mr Zhao Ziyang** then **Mr Zhao**. In Hong Kong the more common practice is to separate the personal names with a hyphen and use lower case for the third character: **Mr Martin Lee Chu-min**.

In Taiwan people (under US influence) often bring the personal name to the front: **Mr Yaobang Hu** then **Mr Hu**; **Mr Edward Chen** then **Mr Chen**.

The FT has adopted the Pinyin style for spelling names, replacing the Wade-Giles system.

Some common names:

Beijing	Guangzhou *not Canton*
Deng Xiaoping	Li Peng
Guangdong	Mao Zedong
Tianjin	Zhao Ziyang
Xinjiang	Zhu Rongji

Chouf Mountains are in Lebanon.

Christian name Beware of using this when writing about people in non-Christian countries. **First name** may be more appropriate.

Christies International has no apostrophe; **Christie's Europe** has one.

churches take capitals for a specific denomination: **the Catholic Church, Protestant, Buddhist** etc; lower case for a building: **St Margaret's church.** *See also* **capitals; churchmen.**

churchmen
   archbishops At first reference write **the archbishop of Canterbury, Dr George Carey,** then write **Dr Carey** or **the archbishop.** Similarly **the archbishop of Westminster, Cardinal Basil Hume;** then **Cardinal Hume.**

   bishops At first reference: **the bishop of Durham, the Rt Rev David Jenkins;** then **Dr Jenkins** or **the bishop.** A Roman Catholic bishop: **the bishop of Casterbridge, Mgr John Brown,** then **Mgr Brown.**

   other ministers At first reference: **the Rev John Green;** then write **Mr Green,** not **Rev Green;** or **Fr John Green,** then **Fr Green.** Write **clergy** not **clergymen.**

Cincinnati, city in Ohio; note the spelling.

cipher is preferred to **cypher.**

circumstances While **in the circumstances** may be preferable, there is nothing inherently wrong with **under the circumstances.**

Ciskei, a South African "homeland" for Xhosa people in the eastern Cape.

Citizen's Charter has initial capitals and refers to a single citizen.

City In the London edition of the FT, references to **the City** are acceptable when writing about London's financial community; in the International Edition some further explanation should be given.

civil servants and the **civil service** are lower case.

claim has come to take the place of **assert**; consider whether this should be so.

clear Avoid the word when you mean something which is not obvious but can be inferred: **The TUC in a clear change of policy agreed to composite the controversial motions 214, 237 and 286.**

clichés, metaphors and tired language

"Our writers are full of clichés, just as old barns are full of bats. There is obviously no rule about this, except that anything you suspect of being a cliché undoubtedly is one and had better be removed."

(Wolcott Gibbs quoted in James Thurber, *The Years with Ross*, 1959).

There is a tabloid world that does not concern the FT journalist. No FT subeditor will be called on to consider a **bishop in love tangle**, which may have left him **flushed with shame**; nor a story about a **heartbreak mum**, possibly caused by her **luscious** daughter's **drugs hell**, brought on by a battle over her **love-tug child**; no one is **over the moon**, nor are they **as sick as a parrot**.

But there are still far too many overworked words and phrases in the pages of the FT, and by a **miracle of modern science** – feeding words into the Profile database – it is possible to discover exactly how overused these words are.

Thus during the sample period (one year's issues of the paper) there were seven **villains of the piece** (not all in opera reviews, surely), nine people who **patched together a compromise**, 45 who **hammered out** something, probably an agreement, 20 who put something **up for grabs**, 28 who found it **crystal clear**, 95 who went **back to square one**, 161 who played a **key role**, 86 of them **at this moment in time**; 145 saw a **green light**, 135 were **beleaguered**, while 33 **sent shock waves** through something, 31 were **tight-lipped**, 27 events **surprised the City** but only four **shocked** it; happily only six were **street-fighters** but 52 found themselves **in the firing line**. In 49 instances something was **psychologically important** (probably an index **rocketing** (51) through a certain point), doubtless **cold comfort** (30) for those 20 who had **played a waiting game**, as 45 were **quick to point out**.

The record was impeccable concerning **iron resolution** and **salami tactics**; much less so in the overuse of **bonanza** (97), **boom** (910), **bottom line** (223), **breakthrough** (418), **clampdown** (87), **circles** (287), **crisis** (a massive 6,472), **crackdown** (293), **cutbacks** (148, should be cuts), **defuse/d** (191, only four of which referred to bombs), **dramatic** (1,224), **elite** (269), **fuel/led** (2,020), **giant** (852), **hit back** (104), **huge** (2,157), **key** (3,493), **massive** (1,028), **meaningful** (168), **overall** (3,593), **prestigious** (164), **problem** (5,122), **run-up** (to an election possibly, 1,889), **saw** (...profits rise; uncountable), **scandal** (609), **slump** (909), **sources** (1,446), **track record** (142), **unprecedented** (617) and **unveil/ed** (900).

In addition there were 657 uses of **prior to**, 656 of which could probably have been replaced by **before**, the other being the head of a religious order (**he asked the prior to pray for him**...); 229 of **per annum** and 277 of **per capita**, where **a year** and **a head** would have been better; 279 references to **persons** (were they not **people**?); 584 to **players**, very few of them members of sports teams; 180 to **planes**, most of them probably aircraft; and 24 uses of the word **schizophrenic**, none used in the correct sense as referring to a specific illness.

Metaphors are to be encouraged but easily succumb to overuse. Some are so striking as to be unrepeatable:

He had all the charm of a steel puddler's underpants

(Raymond Chandler)

The skies over Italy are dark with the wings of chicken come home to roost
(Rupert Cornwell)

Subeditors should be vigilant: if the phrase is tired, lay it to rest. Beware, too, of mixed metaphors:

There are a lot of hiccups still to be ironed out is engaging but nonsense. **The CDU's trump card for the elections is public indignation at the rising tide of asylum-seeking and immigration** might result in a wet pack.

climate is fine for describing the weather, but a cliché in other contexts.

close or **closure**, not **close down**.

closed shop is an agreement between a company and a trade union under which someone may not be employed unless a member of that union; a **post-entry** closed shop forces a worker to join the union.

cold war, referring to the rivalry between the US and the Soviet Union, is lower case.

collective nouns are usually singular. Companies, firms, countries and most organisations are always singular: **Marks and Spencer is launching**; **the government has proclaimed**; **Hamptons is selling**; **the Maldives is to protest**; **Peat Marwick was not informed**.

It is best to avoid phrases such as **accountants Peat Marwick was**...

The same rule applies to what appear to be plural sciences: **politics is**...; **economics is**...; **acoustics is**....

The main exceptions to the rule are sports teams and the police: **England have beaten the West Indies; the police are baffled**.

However, collectives such as family, clergy, committee and parliament should be regarded as singular when unity is intended and plural when the idea of plurality predominates: **The clergy are underpaid** (ie, the members of the clergy) but **the clergy is angry over claims**...(the clergy as a body); **the council was elected** (as a body) but **the council are undecided about the council tax** (the individual members disagreeing).

Note also: **Half the consignment was rotten**; but **half the apples were rotten**. In these instances the plural noun is the determining factor.

Similarly: **none of the apples were eaten**, but **none of the cheese was eaten**.

Where the word **number** is the subject, treat it as singular with a definite article: **The number is estimated at**...; and plural with an indefinite article: **A large number were present**.

Colombia is a South American republic; **British Columbia** is a Canadian province; **District of Columbia (DC)** is a federal district of the eastern US including Washington.; **Colombo** is the capital of Sri Lanka.

coloured *see* **bias.**

combated not **combatted.**

commandos is the plural of **commando.**

commas *see* **stops.**

common sense is two words as a noun, one as an adjective.

Commonwealth of Independent States (CIS) consists of members of the former Soviet union. A list of member states is on page 215.

communist *see* **capitals.**

community charge is the correct name for what was usually called the **poll tax.** *See also* **council tax.**

company names Companies and firms are singular: **ICI has**...; **Marks and Spencer is**....

    Ltd, plc, Inc, SA, et Cie, GmbH, AG, SpA and their equivalents are not used except where it is necessary to distinguish between parent and subsidiary companies.

    The word **firm** is used to describe a professional partnership such as a firm of accountants, solicitors or stockbrokers; also to describe a small business. It is not used as a synonym for company.

    A conglomerate is a group with diversified interests, often built up by acquisition. A multinational is a company that has manufacturing bases or subsidiaries in several countries.

    Company names including initials are written as if they were personal names: **W.H. Smith** not WHSmith; **J.P. Morgan** not JPMorgan, **BHS** not BhS. *See also* **names and titles.**

    Where a company name consists of initials but is pronounced as a word it is printed in upper and lower case: **Citic, Daf, Enserch.** Where the name is pronounced as individual letters it remains in capitals: **BAT, ICI, IMI.** Commas between names are omitted: **Sears Roebuck** not Sears, Roebuck. Middle capitals are usually ignored: **Next Computer** not NeXT. Exceptions are **NatWest, SmithKline Beecham.**

Some confusing company names (and their shortened form in parentheses):

3i

Aérospatiale

BHS *not* B*h*S

Allied-Lyons

American Telephone and
  Telegraph (AT&T)

Anglo American

B&Q

Bayerische Hypotheken- und
  Wechsel-Bank

Bloomingdale's

Boots

Bouygues

Cable and Wireless (C&W)

Campbell Soup

Cheseborough-Pond's

McDonald's *fast foods*

McDonnell Douglas

Mercedes-Benz

Messerschmitt-Bölkow-Blohm
  (MBB)

Moët & Chandon

J.P. Morgan

Moody's

Next Computer *not NeXT*

Océ-van der Grinten

Olympia & York (O&Y)

Pathe Communications *no accent*

P&O [Peninsular and Oriental
  Steam Navigation]

Pan Am

Philips *electronics group*

Phillips *American oil company*

PKbanken

Pratt & Whitney (P&W)

CL-Alexanders Laing &
  Cruikshank

Coca-Cola

Daimler-Benz

de Havilland

Haagen-Dazs

Hamleys

Harrisons & Crosfield

Harrods

Hongkong and Shanghai Bank

Hudson's Bay

Kohlberg Kravis Roberts (KKR)

Lloyds *bank*

Lloyd's *insurance market*

Marks and Spencer (M&S)

Marsh & McLennan

Procter & Gamble

Ranks Hovis McDougall (RHM)

Reckitt & Colman

Rémy Martin

Rolls-Royce *aircraft engines*

Rolls-Royce Motors

Rowe & Pitman

Sears Roebuck *no comma*

Shearson Lehman Hutton

W.H. Smith

SmithKline Beecham

Standard & Poor's

Thorn EMI

Toys R Us

Trans World Airlines (TWA)

Trusthouse Forte (THF)

UBS Phillips & Drew (P&D)

S.G. Warburg

Wärtsilä

compare with not **compare to** unless similarity is intended. **Shall I compare thee to a summer's day?**

compass points are hyphenated and lower case: **north-west, south-east**. *See also* **capitals**.

complement is to complete, set off: **compliment** is to praise.

compose means to put together, make up by combining: **comprise** means to include, contain, consist of.

composers and other musicians The FT follows the spelling used in *Grove's Dictionary of Music and Musicians*, with a few exceptions. This means that Tchaikovsky is now correct. Note also **Rakhmaninov** and **Skryabin**; but **Schnittke** not **Shnitke**. *See also* **music**; **opera titles**; **Russian names**.

compound means to mix together, settle or condone. It does not mean to multiply or complicate.

comprise means to be composed of; it refers to all the components of something; it does not take **of**: **Six quartets comprise Haydn's Opus 77** or **Haydn's Opus 77 consists of six quartets**; but not **Haydn's Opus 77 is comprised of six quartets**.

congressmen/women are members of the US Congress (House of Representatives). Use lower case for **congressional**. *See also* **capitals**.

consensus is an overused word; **agreement** may be better.

Conservatives in the UK can also be called **Tories**.

constituency is a body of voters, not a body of support. Prefer **supporters** to the American sense of **constituency**.

consortia is the plural of **consortium**.

Consumers' Association has an apostrophe; it is the publisher of **Which?**, which has a question mark.

contemporary means at the time of an event or person being written about; not at the time of the user of the word. It usually means **then** not

now. A production of *A Midsummer Night's Dream* with contemporary incidental music has music by a composer of Shakespeare's time.

contempt of court *see* **law and libel**, pages 189–192.

Continent can be used to mean the Continent of Europe; other continents should be lower case.

continual is repeated over a period of time; **continuous** means uninterrupted.

controversial appeared 1,271 times in a sample year's FTs: too often.

convince does not mean **persuade**. **The prime minister was persuaded** (not convinced) **to call an autumn election**, though he may have been convinced of the wisdom of doing so.

co-operate, co-operative are hyphenated; uncooperative is not. In the UK the movement consists of the **Co-operative Wholesale Society, Co-operative Insurance Society** and **Co-operative party**.
   Other words with **co** prefixes are hyphenated only if two **o's** would abut: **coaxial, co-ordinate**.

Córdoba, Argentine province and city, Spanish city, Colombian province, all named after the Spanish explorer; do not use the English spelling **Cordova**.

Corporation of London is the local authority for the City of London, usually called the **City Corporation**. A full meeting is the **Court of Common Council**.

Côte d'Ivoire, West African republic, used to be called the **Ivory Coast**.

council tax is the UK government's replacement for the **community charge** or **poll tax** *qv*.

countries are neuter not female. A list of some states, provinces, counties and regions is on pages 214–220.

courts In England and Wales **magistrates' courts** deal with most minor criminal offences; more serious cases are heard in a **crown court** presided over by circuit judges, some of whom are also High Court judges. There are 94 crown courts, the best known being the **Central Criminal Court**, generally known as the **Old Bailey**.

Civil cases are heard in **county courts** (270) and in the **High Court**. The High Court has three divisions: **Queen's Bench Division, Chancery Division, Family Division**.

Appeals are heard in the **Court of Appeal** (never appeal court). They are presided over by **lords justices of appeal** (who, like High Court judges, are knights), headed by the **Master of the Rolls** (civil cases) or the **Lord Chief Justice** (Court of Appeal, Criminal Division).

Further appeals are to the House of Lords, where they are heard by **lords of appeal** (who are life peers), commonly referred to as **law lords**. Write **the law lords ruled**... or **the House of Lords ruled**...

The head of the judiciary in England and Wales (and Speaker of the House of Lords) is the **Lord Chancellor**.

Lawyers' titles should usually be in lower case **(the magistrate, counsel for Mr Grey, the coroner)**, except when used as a personal title **(Judge Brown, Mr Justice Black, Lord Justice Green)**. Queen's Counsel take the abbreviation **QC** after the name without an intervening comma: **Mr John White QC**.

The senior judge of the Chancery Division is the **Vice-Chancellor**. The first reference to him in copy should be **Sir Donald Nicholls, the Vice-Chancellor**. Thereafter he should be referred to as **Sir Donald** or **the judge**.

High Court judges should first be referred to as **Mr Justice Black**, thereafter as the judge. A High Court judge should never be referred to as **Judge Black**. Similarly **Lord Justice Green** can after first reference be called **the judge**.

Some High Court cases are heard by County Court judges sitting as judges of the High Court, who should be referred to as **Judge Brown**, or by QCs, sitting as deputy High Court judges, who should be referred to as **Deputy Judge John White QC** and then as **the judge**.

Writs, which start civil legal actions, are issued not taken out. Similarly an injunction is **granted**, not taken out.

The **European Court** is shorthand for the **European Court of Justice**, the EC court which sits at Luxembourg. It should not be confused with the **European Court of Human Rights**, which is associated with the Council of Europe and sits in Strasbourg.

In FT Law Reports, names of cases are usually in capitals; names of counsel appear at the end in italics.

Court reporting is a specialised art: FT journalists can seek advice from the law courts reporter or legal correspondent if they are in any doubt about the accuracy of what they have written.

credible is believable; **credulous** tending to believe something.

crematoria is the plural of **crematorium**.

crescendo means getting louder, not a high point or climax; plural is **crescendos**.

crisis is a crucial stage or turning point; an unstable period of extreme trouble or danger. Beware of writing **crisis** when you mean anything less than this. A crisis cannot grow or worsen.

Cruft's is the dog show.

cruise is the missile (lower case because it cruises); contrast **Pershing**, which has a capital **P**.

curate's egg In the famous Punch cartoon the curate replied to the bishop: "Oh no, my lord, it's excellent in parts." In fact the curate's egg was rotten all through. Avoid the phrase unless making a subtle point.
See also **Hobson's choice**.

currencies In the London edition of the FT the first currency figure should be converted into pounds sterling: **DM45bn (£18.4bn)**. In the International edition the conversion should be made into dollars.
Currencies are expressed as: **£1; £2,000–£3,000; £2bn–£3bn; $10.20; 50 cents**. There is no space between a currency symbol and the figure that follows, except with the Dutch florin, where a thin space should separate the two.
Refer to currencies in text as the French franc, the Canadian dollar, etc. But note that the German currency is the D-Mark in text.
A list of the main world currencies is on pages 158–163.

currently **Now** or **at present** might be better, but the word can usually be omitted.

curriculums is the preferred plural of **curriculum**.

curtainraiser is a story filed before an event, outlining the timetable, probable outcome, etc.

cut rather than **cut back**.

Czechoslovak is the adjective from Czechoslovakia. Former Czechoslovakia is now divided into the **Czech Republic** and **Slovakia** or the **Slovak Republic**.

D

Dahomey in West Africa is now called **Benin**.

Dakar is the capital of Senegal; **Dhaka** is the capital of Bangladesh.

Dáil Eireann is the lower house of the Irish parliament, usually called the **Dáil**.

damp Fires or expectations are **damped down**, not **dampened down**.

Dar es Salaam is the capital of Tanzania.

dashes *see* **brackets**.

data show, not shows; a plural noun.

datelines *see* **bylines**.

dates FT style for writing dates is **June 23 1994** (no commas, month/date/year), **August 17, September 12–24 1994, November 25–December 5 1994, January 1994**.

Note:
> In the US 1.9.94 is January 9 1994.
> Decades are written **the 1920s, the 1860s, 1993–94** (not **1993–4** or **1993/94**); also **a woman in her 50s**.
> **Twentieth century** is written out.
> Dates should be given where possible: **last month** can easily cause confusion, especially when the story is put into the Profile database and a time lapse occurs.
> **Prewar** and **postwar** are not hyphenated.
> Names of months should not be abbreviated except in tables.
> BC should appear after the numbers to which it refers: **65–5BC**; AD should only be used for dates before **AD1000**.

dawn raid occurs when a buyer tries to acquire a large block of shares in one swoop, normally at the start of a day's trading. It is used to build up a strategic shareholding, often before a takeover bid.

debacle needs no accents.

decimals always retain the zero before a decimal point **(0.6** not **.6)**. The only exception is for gun calibre: **.303, .22,** etc.

In currency conversions the converted figure should normally be written to the same number of decimal places as the figure converted.

Note: In many other countries figures and dates are written differently: a decimal comma is used, meaning that **1.0763** would be expressed as **1,0763**. *See also* **fractions**.

decimate can be used to mean **destroy** or **kill a large proportion of**. Its original meaning was to kill or destroy one in ten (mutineers, etc) in the Roman army.

decorations Normally the only mention of decorations in the FT is when recording the twice-yearly honours list. Remember that someone is **appointed** an OBE etc, not awarded one.

defamation *see* **law and libel**, pages 189–192.

definite means certain, precise; **definitive** means conclusive, final. A definitive offer is the last word.

deliver is transitive: goods and babies are delivered. It should not be used as an intransitive verb.

a dependant is **dependent** on the person whose **dependant** she is.

depository is a store; **a depositary** is someone with whom something is entrusted.

deprecate is to express disapproval; **depreciate** is to reduce in value.

desiccate has one **s** and two **c's**.

despite Prefer **in spite of**.

detente is the easing of tension between nations; no accent.

detrimental Possibly **harmful** would be better.

Deutschemark is referred to as the **D-Mark** in text and as **DM100m** in figures.

devaluation How to calculate a devaluation in percentage terms:

The Peruvian inte was 700 to the $, and is now 920. Deduct 700 from 920 = 220. Divide 220 by 920 and multiply by 100 to get the percentage devaluation = 23.91, which in a news story can be rounded up to 24 per cent.

The formula is:

$$\frac{\textbf{New figure minus old figure}}{\textbf{New figure}} \times \textbf{100}$$

or in this case: **(920 − 700) × 100/920 = 23.91**

Another example: There were eight Utopian zombies to the £, now there are 10. 10 − 8 = 2. Divide by 10. It equals a 20 per cent devaluation. The point to remember is that it is worked out on the basis of the new figure, not the old.

An alternative method is to divide the old figure by the new and subtract 1; then multiply by 100:

$$\textbf{[(700/920) − 1] × 100 = 23.91}$$

This method saves two calculator keystrokes.

Currency devaluations can *never* reach 100 per cent, let alone exceed it. 100 per cent means the currency is being given away, more than that, you get free dollars thrown in.

Dhahran is a town in Saudi Arabia.

different to Common usage prefers **different from**; however, there is nothing grammatically wrong with the phrase **different to**. **Different than** is common in the US; it should be resisted.

dilemma is not just a difficulty; it is to be faced with two (only two) alternative courses of action, both undesirable.

disc is the spelling used for records or computer discs (not disk).

discomfit is to overwhelm or utterly defeat; **discomfort** is to make uncomfortable.

discreet means tactful, careful to avoid embarrassment; **discrete** means separate or distinct.

disinterested means neutral, unbiased or impartial; it does not mean uninterested. However, in modern English disinterested is often used where uninterested is meant; resist this.

dispensable not -ible.

dispatch is preferred to **despatch**, noun and verb.

distinct means clear, precise, different; **distinctive** means characteristic.

divergent means moving further apart; it does not mean different.

Djibouti is a country in east Africa.

Dnepr is a river in Russia; prefer this spelling to **Dnieper**.

doctors In the FT the title **Dr** has been reserved for physicians, doctors of divinity and archbishops. This rule can now be relaxed where **Dr** is the accepted title of someone in his or her normal working life. The same rule

applies to professors, who should be called **Professor Bloggs** first, then **Prof Bloggs**. But try to keep Prof for genuine chair-holding professors.

Many people in public life on the Continent of Europe have cumbersome titles. Prefer **Mr/Mrs/Ms** in most instances.

Dominica is one of the Windward Islands in the Caribbean; the **Dominican Republic** is the eastern half of Hispaniola, an island in the Caribbean; the western half is Haiti.

down may be a preposition, an adverb, an adjective and a noun; it should not be used as a verb, especially when referring to aircraft. Prefer **shot down** or a similar phrase.

doyen/ne is used to refer to the senior member of a group, profession or society. It does not just mean highly respected.

dramatic What is dramatic to an economist is not necessarily so to anyone else. Beware.

drink types of wine are printed in roman type and lower case: **amontillado, armagnac, bordeaux, burgundy, calvados, champagne, cognac, fino, manzanilla, sauternes**.

Names of grapes should have an initial capital: **Chardonnay, Muller-Thurgau, Sauvignon, Syrah, Zinfandel**.

Names of specific wines should be capitalised: **Marlborough Chardonnay, Château Mouton-Rothschild, Côte de Beaune, Chablis Grand Cru, Krug Grande Cuvée Brut, Cockburn's Special Reserve, Wehlener Sonnenuhr Riesling Kabinett, Domecq's Rio Viejo, Sylvaner Zotzenberg**. Note that accents should be used where appropriate.

Most other wine terms should be printed in roman type, lesser known words and phrases in italics; capitals should be retained where they would be used in the original language: **Appellation Contrôlée, Auslese, bianco, brut, classico, cru bourgeois, cru classé, cuvée, département, grand cru, Halbtrocken, Kabinett, méthode champenoise, premier cru, secco, Société Anonyme, Spätlese, spumante, Trockenbeerenauslese, vin ordinaire, vin de pays**.

Use italics only for terms that are likely to be quite unfamiliar to the reader or where you wish to emphasise the "foreignness" of a word and where logic would suggest that a straight translation might be appropriate: *négociant* is an example, a term that means somewhat more than negotiator.

Do not, however, use a foreign word where an accurate English translation is available.

Remember that **whisky** is Scotch, **whiskey** may be Irish or rye or bourbon.

drowned does not require the word **was**, unless someone else was responsible.

Druze an Islamic sect in Syria and Lebanon, living usually in the mountains.

due to A payment is **due to** someone; do not use **due to** when you mean **because of**.

Dumbarton is a town in western Scotland; **Dunbarton** was a county in western Scotland until 1975, when it became part of Strathclyde.

Dunkirk is not yet spelt **Dunkerque** in the FT.

Düsseldorf, German city, has an Umlaut on the **u**; if this is not available, spell it **Duesseldorf**.

Dutch and Flemish names **den** and **van** are in lower case in Dutch names: **Mr Joop den Uyl, Mr den Uyl**; but in capitals in Flemish (Belgian) names: **Mr Karel Van Miert, Mr Van Miert**. Residents of Dutch Flanders usually follow the Dutch rules.

dwarfs is the plural of **dwarf**, except in *The Lord of the Rings*.

dynamoes is the plural of **dynamo**.

E

Earls Court exhibition centre has no apostrophe; the place itself is losing its own.

earth is lower case unless it is used with names of other planets.

earthquakes are measured on the **Richter scale** *qv*.

EC is the abbreviation for the **European Community**; it should be used only when referring to the Community before the creation of the **European Union** in 1993, or when writing about EC institutions and legislation that has not changed since then. The **European Commission** can be called **Brussels** in headlines.

echoes is the plural of echo; but note the French newspaper **Les Echos**.

ecology is the study of plants, animals or people in relation to the environment. It is not synonymous with **environment**.

economics is a singular noun: **economics is a waste of time**; **economical** means money-saving, thrifty.

Ecu is the **European Currency Unit**; in figures **Ecu20bn**. It is a currency based on a basket weighted according to each country's share of EU output.

Ecuador in South America; note the spelling of **Ecuadorean**.

editorialising The line dividing news stories, ie the reporting of facts, from features incorporating judgments is sometimes blurred.

Writers should ensure that their own opinions do not intrude: **The Ruritanians reacted with predictable anger**... The anger may be predictable to someone who has been following the story, but not necessarily to anyone unfamiliar with these events.

In 1991 the EC's social charter was described in a news item as **infamous**.

Whatever the writer's views on the charter, an opinion such as this should not have appeared in a news story.

Another story started:

The EU yesterday recognised San Serife and Bodoni, albeit with understandable caveats from France and the UK.

Why should these caveats be **understandable** to the reader? the writer has not yet explained them. Perhaps the author was trying to say to the reader: "I am clever enough to know that France and the UK would object."

education **Pupils** study in schools, **students** in universities and colleges. Common examinations are **A levels** and **GCSE**. Examinations can become **exams** in headings.

Make sure you are correct when writing about **state schools, independent schools, grammar schools, public schools, grant-assisted schools**. The structure of the British educational system is changing fast.

effectively means with effect. An **effective** scheme is one that achieves its objective; a company that is **in effect** bankrupt is as good as bankrupt but not technically so. **Effective power** is tautologous: power is not power unless it is effective.

Eire should not be used in referring to the **Irish Republic**.

electrocution results in death; do not confuse it with **electric shock**.

embargoes is the plural of **embargo**.

embarrass is often misspelt.

employ Use may be better.

enable Avoid writing **enable** where you mean **allow**.

encyclopedia is preferred to **encyclopaedia**.

enormity is something monstrous or wicked; it has nothing to do with size: **The enormity of the scam perpetrated by Robert Maxwell**... is correct use of the word.

enquire, enquiry Prefer **inquire, inquiry**.

enrol has one **l**; but note **enrolled, enrolment**.

eponymous is the sort of word that makes the writer seem learned; many readers will not know what it means. Avoid it.

escalate means to increase step by step; do not use it only to mean rise or develop.

Eskimo **Inuit** or **Innu** are now preferred to Eskimo.

ethnic refers to race or nationality but has almost come to be a synonym for **exotic** or **foreign**. In the US it can be a noun, meaning a member of an ethnic minority.

ethnic cleansing refers to the forcible removal of one ethnic group from land claimed by another; it has been used as a euphemism for the mass expulsion and killing of rival groups, especially in former Yugoslavia. The phrase should not be used unqualified or unexplained; preferably it should be confined to direct quotes from participants in conflicts.

EU is the abbreviation for the **European Union**, which was formed as a result of the **Maastricht treaty** in 1993; it can also be called the **Union** for variation.

euphemism *see* **formal words; jargon; political correctness**.

Euro-MP is acceptable in headlines for a member of the European Parliament; in text prefer **MEP**.

Europe is the entire continent including Britain; do not confuse it with the **EC** or with **western Europe** or with the **Continent**.

ex- is best avoided: **former president** is better than **ex-president**; and there is no right way to hyphenate **ex prime minister**.

exceptional means out of the ordinary; **exceptionable** means open to objection.

execute Terrorists kill, murder or shoot their victims; they do not execute them. Courts sentence to execution.

expletives The FT has no strict policy. However, the gratuitous use of expletives or obscenities is discouraged. The test to apply is whether they add anything to the story.

Four letter expletives will usually be confined to infrequent use in the review pages.

The word wanker has appeared only once in the FT; it was a misprint for banker.

extravert not **extrovert**.

eyewitness **Witness** is usually enough.

F

facelift is one word.

Falkland Islands can also be called **the Falklands**.

Far East is often too vague a description; write **South Asia, East Asia, South-East Asia**, etc.

Faroe Islands/Faroes are Atlantic islands between Shetland and Iceland; this spelling is preferred to **Faeroes**.

farther is used when referring to distance; **further** means additionally.

Fascist should be capitalised only when referring to a political party; in other instances use lower case.

fatwa is a formal legal opinion delivered by an Islamic religious leader. It is not necessarily a sentence of death or punishment. The word came into prominence following Ayatollah Khomeini's fatwa in 1989 over Salman Rushdie's book *The Satanic Verses*.

faux pas The plural is the same.

feasible means capable of being done, not **probable** or **plausible**.

females, feminism *see* **bias**.

fetid is preferred to the variant **foetid**.

fewer refers to numbers: **fewer books, fewer children**. Less refers to quantity: **less than £100, less than a quarter**.
     However, there is no overwhelming argument for writing **fewer than two years** or **no fewer than 15 minutes; less than two years, no less than 15 minutes** are acceptable; **no fewer than** tends to look pedantic.

fiascos is the plural of **fiasco**.

figures Numbers **one** to **nine** and ordinals **first** to **ninth** are spelt out. Use figures for **10** and over and in conjunction with units of measurement (**1 mile, 2 per cent, 9am, 100ha**); also for fractions (**2½ months**) or decimals (**2.5**) and ordinals (**18th century**). Use figures for a range of numbers such as **9–12 months**.

Fractions are hyphenated when written out: **two-thirds**. Do not mix fractions with decimals, except when following convention in some markets stories.

Do not start a sentence with a figure. Write the number in words or rephrase the sentence.

Millions: **1m, 6.3m, 1.63m** (preferred to **1,630,000**); **500,000** is preferable to ½m.

Billions: A billion is 1,000 million; **2bn, 14.8bn**.

Trillions: A trillion is a million million, but is best avoided: **2,000bn** is preferable to **2 trillion**.

Ranges: Write **£5m–£10m, 10,000–12,000, 3m–4m**; not **£5–10m, 10–12,000, 3–4m**; however, **3–4 per cent** is acceptable. **Estimates ranged between £2m and £3m**, not **between £2m–£3m**.

Write **a head** rather than **per capita**; **a year** rather than **per annum**.

In text always write **per cent**; the % sign should be used in headlines.

Write ratios (eg votes) as **nine to four, 55 to 48**; but a **24–20 vote** is acceptable.

Write **from 1926 to 1928** or in **1926–28**, not **from 1926–28**; write **between 1926 and 1928** not **between 1926–28**.

filibuster is the process of delaying legislation by means of long speeches and other tactics.

Filipino is an inhabitant of the **Philippines**.

film titles should be printed in italics; use initial capitals, except for conjunctions, articles, prepositions, etc: *Raiders of the Lost Ark*.

fiord not **fjord**.

firefighter is more accurate than **fireman**. *See also* **bias**.

firm is normally used to describe partnerships: stockbrokers, accountants, solicitors, etc. Otherwise write **company, concern, group, business**. However, **small firm** is now in common use and may be used as a variant.

first not firstly, **second** not secondly.

first world war is now all lower case.

flaunt is to display ostentatiously; **flout** is to show contempt for.

flu, short for influenza, needs no apostrophe.

focuses has two **s's** not three; note **focused** not **focussed**.

foetus not **fetus**.

following After is a shorter word and is preferred.

Fontainebleau in northern France, famous for its palace; note the spelling.

food Use roman type in lower case where an item or dish is likely to be familiar to readers: **antipasto, béarnaise, bistro, foie gras, matzos, mousseline, pot au feu, ravioli, rouille, roux, tagliatelle, vichyssoise, vinaigrette**.

Food named after places takes a capital where the connection is still strong: **Double Gloucester, Stilton, Worcestershire sauce**; but lower case where the connection has loosened or where the names have become generic: **Canadian cheddar, German brie**.

Use italics for unfamiliar names and cooking terms which might lose their flavour in translation: *à point, au bleu, moules et frites, nouvelle cuisine, le saumon au champagne* or masterpieces such as those created by Aunt's Dahlia's chef Anatole; *Sylphides à la creme d'ecrevisses, Timbales de ris de veau toulousaines*. Bertie Wooster's other recollections of Anatole's cooking **(Les fried smelts, Le Bird of some kind with chipped potatoes, Le ice cream)** can remain in roman type, as can most menu items.

Do not be pretentious: write **smoked salmon** rather than *saumon fumé*.

forbear is to abstain; **forebear** is an ancestor.

forego is to precede; **forgo** is to do without.

foreign names *see* **Arab and Persian, Burmese, Chinese, Dutch, German, Indonesian, Korean, Malaysian, Portuguese, Spanish, Thai, Turkish names**.

foreign words Avoid foreign words if an English alternative is available. Write **a head** rather than **per capita; a year** or **yearly** rather than **per annum**.
   Some foreign words and phrases are printed in italics; a larger number have been anglicised and should be printed in roman type. Lists are printed in the entry under **italics**.
   If you use a foreign word make sure it is spelt and accented correctly.

forensic means belonging to courts of law. It does not mean medical. Forensic medicine is medical jurisprudence.

formal words should be avoided if possible.

Avoid	*Prefer*
accommodate	hold, contain
amidst	amid
amongst	among
anticipate	expect *usually*
as a result of	because
approximately	about

assistance	help
cease	stop
commence	begin, start
conceal	hide
conservative *estimate*	low, safe
confrontation	dispute
demonstrate	show
discontinue	stop
donate	give
endeavour	try
establish	set up
facilitate	ease
facility	plant
following	after
high-ranking	senior
in addition	also
in short supply	scarce
inform	tell
initiate	start
lengthy	long
loaned	lent
manufacture	make
materialise	happen, appear
necessity	need
negotiations	talks
numerous	many
objective	aim
obtain	get
overwhelming	big, clear
participate	take part
partially	partly
per annum	a year
permit	help
personnel	workers, staff
persons	people
prior to	before
purchase	buy
request	ask
requirements	needs
revealed	said

stated	said
subsequently	after, later
substantial	big
sufficient	enough
sustain	suffer
transportation	transport
whilst	while

former and **latter** are best avoided because they often interrupt the flow by making the reader's eyes refer backwards in the sentence when they should be moving forwards.

formulas is the preferred plural of **formula**.

fortuitous means accidental; it should not be confused with **fortunate**.

forums is the plural of **forum**.

fourth estate is the press; the first three are the lords, commons and clergy.

fractions and decimals Figures are normally expressed in decimals in the text of the newspaper. It is important not to mix decimals and fractions in the same story; but interest rates are often quoted in fractions of a percentage point and should not be converted to decimals.

Prices on the London Stock Exchange and exchanges in the US and Canada are quoted in fractions of a dollar or a penny and should not be changed. Exchanges in the Far East, Australasia and on the continent of Europe quote prices in decimals.

When fractions are spelt out they should be hyphenated: **two-thirds**. *See also* **decimals**.

Frankfurt am Main is a city in west Germany; **Frankfurt an der Oder** is a city in east Germany near the Polish border.

fraught means filled or charged with. A question can be fraught with difficulties. This does not make it a fraught question.

frescoes is the plural of **fresco**.

front bench is two words but **frontbencher** is one.

fulfil, **fulfilled**, **fulfilment** Note spellings.

fulsome has a pejorative meaning: excessive or insincere. It does not mean lavish. The word fulsome appeared 20 times in a sample year's issues of the FT: in every instance it was wrongly used.

A few examples:

While Mr Clarke is fulsome in his praise of Lord White...

The moves came after Mr Helmut Kohl issued a statement of fulsome tribute and thanks to President Mikhail Gorbachev.

Ron Todd received a warm display of affection from delegates and a fulsome eulogy from Bill Morris.

Official Torydom paid fulsome tributes. Mr Patten described his former leader as one of the greatest prime ministers in British history.

It may be that in the last example the word was used in its correct sense; but I doubt it.

Fujeirah is a member of the United Arab Emirates.

Fujiyama or **Mount Fuji** is an extinct volcano in central Japan; do not write **Mount Fujiyama**.

future **In the near future** could well be **soon**.

G

Gaborone is the capital of Botswana.

Gadaffi **Colonel Muammer Gadaffi** is the Libyan head of state; various spellings exist but the FT prefers **Gadaffi**.

the Gambia is a country in West Africa; note the lower case **the**.

gaol is wrong, **jail** is correct.

Garda, Gardai, the Irish police: **a Garda spokesman said...; Gardai in Dublin said...**

gas field is two words; **oilfield** is one.

gay It is better to write **homosexual** if that is what you mean. Remember that homosexual refers to both sexes.

gender is a set of two or more grammatical categories into which the nouns of some languages are divided; unfortunately it is also being increasingly used where the word **sex** would be more accurate: **Her gender impressed White House operatives**...; it did not: her sex did.

It may be too late to reverse this trend, especially in such phrases as **gender-typing** or whatever.

general election is lower case.

geniuses is the preferred plural of **genius**.

German names **von** is lower case but is not used when the surname only is used: **Adolf von Spiegelberger, Mr Spiegelberger**.

Germany was reunited on October 3 1990. Write **east Germany** and **west Germany** when referring to the present counterparts of the old East Germany and West Germany. The country is the **Federal Republic of Germany**. The German Democratic Republic no longer exists.

gerrymander (not jerrymander) is to divide a voting area so as to give one party an unfair advantage.

gerunds A gerund is a noun formed from a verb. Its correct use and the use of other words affected is shown in the following examples:

They have been blocked by the objections of farmers to *providing* **suitable land and by the reluctance of local authorities to use powers of compulsory purchase.**

The navy is not equal to *performing* **the task of patrolling the area.**

Mr Clarke is committed to *introducing* **a new tax on singing in public places.**

The long-term investment case for Hydro-Electric and Scottish Power rests on *their* **(not them)** *being seen* **as border reivers.**

We need fear nothing from *China's* **(not China)** *developing* **its resources.**

Gettysburg in Pennsylvania was the site of a crucial battle in the American civil war; the **Gettysburg Address** was made by President Lincoln at the dedication of the national cemetery in 1863.

Ghent is a city in Belgium; Flemish spelling is **Gent**, French spelling **Gand**.

ghettos is the preferred plural of **ghetto**.

giant is what only a very few companies are; avoid it if possible.

global might quite well be **world; global player** is what many companies like to think they are and it is a term to be avoided.

Golders Green in London has no apostrophe.

good and bad What is good for a producer and his profits is not necessarily good for a consumer. Be careful not to identify with the interests of a particular group.

Gorbachev, Mikhail former Soviet and Russian leader; the name is pronounced **-ov** but written **-ev**.

Gothenburg is the English name from the Swedish port **Göteborg**.

government is always lower case. *See* **capitals**.

grammar

> "The vulgar grammar-maker, dazzled by the glory of the ruling language, knew no better than to transfer to English the scheme that belonged to Latin. What chance had our poor mother-tongue in the clutch of this Procrustes?"
>
> > (J.W. Hales, quoted in *Fowler's Modern English Usage*).

Once grammar was treated reverentially, a legacy of the influence of Latin. Now the opposite is true and grammar is often regarded (as Orwell recommended) as "of no importance so long as we make our meaning plain".

We should aim to tread a careful path between colloquialism and fustiness. The fact that teaching in British schools now pays less attention to grammatical principles than, say, 40 years ago, does not absolve the journalist from the duty to write clear and concise English, avoiding ambiguity.

Bear in mind that short words are better than long ones; that the active voice is better than the passive; that if a word can be removed, it should be; that an English word is preferable to a foreign one; that short sentences are easier to understand than long ones; and that slang or jargon should be avoided.

See also **alternative, ampersands, apostrophes, brackets, but, fewer, formal words, gerunds, hyphens, last and past, only, prepositions, quotation marks, reported speech, split infinitives, stops in punctuation, subjunctives, that, which, whose**.

Great Britain is England, Scotland and Wales; write **Britain**. **United Kingdom** is England, Wales, Scotland and Northern Ireland.

green paper, a government discussion document, is lower case. *See* **capitals**.

Gresham's Law "Bad money drives out good": a superior currency will tend to be hoarded and the inferior will dominate the circulation.

grey is a colour; Americans write **gray**.

grisly means gruesome, causing horror; **grizzly** means somewhat grey and is also the spelling of a variety of brown bear.

groundhog is a woodchuck, a North American marmot with coarse reddish-brown fur. US tradition says that if the groundhog in Punxsutawney, Pennsylvania, sees its shadow on February 2, another six weeks of winter will follow.

guerrilla has two **r's** and two **l's**. *See also* **bias**.

Guiana is a region in the north-eastern part of South America, embracing Guyana (formerly British Guiana), Surinam (formerly Dutch Guiana), French Guiana, and small parts of Venezuela and Brazil.

Guinea, formerly French Guinea, and **Guinea-Bissau**, formerly Portuguese Guinea, are adjoining republics in West Africa.

Guildhall in the City of London is just **Guildhall** not the **Guildhall**.

guillotine in the House of Commons is the application of a strict timetable to expedite legislation, which is enforced by a vote after a three-hour debate.

Gujarat is a state in west India; this spelling is preferred to **Gujerat**.

the Gulf is just that, not the Persian Gulf or Arabian Gulf; note the **Gulf war** (lower case **w**).

Gurkhas are Hindus living mainly in Nepal; the plural is **Gurkhas**.

Guyana is a republic in South America, formerly **British Guiana**.

gypsy is preferred to **gipsy**; the **British Gypsy Council** uses this spelling.

H

Haarlem is a city in the Netherlands; **Harlem** is a district of New York City, in Manhattan.

haemorrhage means profuse bleeding and is too often used to refer to the disappearance of cash.

haemorrhoids, a difficult word to spell.

The Hague is the capital of the Netherlands; note the capital **T**.

hajj is the annual Moslem pilgrimage to Mecca, a **haji** is someone who has performed it.

haloes is the plural of **halo**.

halve To write that a population has **more than halved** is not wrong, but less clear than saying that the population has **fallen to less than half**. Half can be singular or plural: **half the votes were counted; half the food was eaten**.

hangar is a building for storing aircraft.

Hanover in Germany; the English spelling has one **n**.

Hapsburg The European royal family; the German name is **Habsburg**.

hara-kiri is ritual suicide in Japan.

harass not **harrass**.

Haringey is a north London borough.

Harrods, the London store, has no apostrophe.

Hawaii is a US state in the central Pacific; the adjective is **Hawaiian**.

headache is a medical condition, not what a company suffers from when its profits fall.

headlines headline writing is an art, not a skill that can be taught within the pages of a house style book. A few general reminders are listed below:

(*a*) Headlines should normally contain a verb, preferably in some form other than the present participle; label heads should be avoided if possible. Queries in heads are forbidden.

(*b*) Make sure that the headline explains what the story is about; preferably take it from the first paragraph of the story, without necessarily reproducing the words of the intro.

(*c*) Single quotes are used in FT heads. Make sure that the quotes reproduce the exact words said.

(*d*) Bear in mind that 40 per cent of FT readers are outside Britain, and avoid headlines such as **Unions vote to strike** or **PM stands firm on election date** unless the page heading makes it clear what country's unions are involved or which prime minister.

(*e*) Aim to make each line a reasonable fit; however, a bit of pink space at the end of a headline aids legibility. Try to make the top line of a two-deck head longer than the second.

(*f*) Try to make the headline phrase line by line since the eye absorbs a line at a time. A second world war splash head read:

French push bottles
up German rear

(*g*) The % sign is used in heads, not per cent written out.

(*h*) Be careful not to confuse principal companies with their subsidiaries.

(*i*) Beware of puns unless they are truly original: **Airline profits lift off** may have been acceptable when first used; by now it and dozens like it, are merely tired. *See also* **puns**.

(*j*) Computer technology allows heads to be squeezed to fit; use these facilities sparingly.

(*k*) Keep short headline words for when you really need them: **ban, bid, claim, cut, hits, move, pact, plea, probe, quit, rush, slash** are all invaluable, but should not be overused.

healthcare is one word, not hyphenated.

healthy (as in **healthy turnover**) should not be used as a synonym for good or profitable.

Heidelberg is a city in Germany.

here should not be used to locate a story; be specific with place of happening. The byline should normally tell the reader where the writer is.

heighten **Raise** is often a better word.

Hercegovina is part of the former Yugoslav province of **Bosnia-Hercegovina**; this spelling is preferred to **Herzegovina**.

hiccup not **hiccough**.

High Court *see* **courts**.

high street, meaning a town's main retailing area, is still acceptable in the London FT, but should be avoided in the International Edition. But bear in mind that retailing is increasingly carried out on industrial estates or in specially built shopping centres.

high-tech is acceptable if **high technology** is spelt out first. **Hi-tech** may be used in heads.

hike is a walk not a rise in salary, or any other rise.

historic means famous in history, **historical** means belonging to history. Do not confuse the two.

HIV is the **human immunodeficiency virus** which may lead to Aids. It is not a disease.

Ho Chi Minh City in Vietnam was formerly **Saigon**.

Hobson's choice means taking what is offered or nothing at all. *See also* **curate's egg**.

Holland consists of two provinces of the Netherlands. Do not write Holland for the country as a whole.

home is not necessarily a synonym for **house**, though those trying to sell them might wish to persuade you otherwise.

home counties of England are Essex, Hertfordshire, Kent and Surrey, but sometimes include Berkshire, Buckinghamshire and Sussex. Avoid the term if there is any doubt, and avoid it entirely in the International Edition by writing **south-east England**.

homelands, the self-governing regions of South Africa set up under apartheid for 10 black tribes.

homogeneous means similar in kind or nature, uniform; **homogenous** means similar because of common ancestry.

homosexual refers to women as well as men.

Hong Kong is two words but beware of companies that are called **Hongkong**...

honours and honorifics Do not use honorifics such as HRH, Hon, Right Hon, Bart, etc, either before or after a name; do not give awards such as VC or qualifications such as MA, ARIBA. Queen's counsel keep their QC: **Mr George Carman QC**.

hopefully should be avoided when used to mean **it is to be hoped that**; it often fails to explain who is doing the hoping and may lead to ambiguity; **fears** should also be treated carefully.

Horserace Totalisator Board is the **Tote**, which can be used at second and later mentions.

houmus is a Middle Eastern dish make from chick peas; sometimes spelt **houmous**.

House of Representatives is the US Congress.

Hudson Bay is the place in Canada, **Hudson's Bay** the company.

huge is best avoided.

hyphens

"If you take hyphens seriously you will surely go mad" (*Anon*)

"No attempt will be made here to describe modern English usage in the matter of hyphens; its infinite variety defies description."

(*Fowler's Modern English Usage*)

No two sets of rules will be found that agree on this subject, so total consistency is unlikely. However, keep the number of hyphens to a minimum; use them only when needed. The *Concise Oxford Dictionary* is not to be trusted on the subject of hyphenation.

As Fowler points out, the hyphen is not an ornament but an aid to understanding: **Bach's 200-odd cantatas** is not the same as **Bach's 200 odd cantatas**.

Although a compound noun such as **build-up** may be hyphenated, do not hyphenate the verb to **build up** or many others like it. Similarly **up-to-date figures** should include hyphens; the **figures are up to date** should not.

Adverbs linked to verbs should not be hyphenated unless there is the risk of ambiguity: **A closely guarded secret** does not need a hyphen, nor does **a wholly owned subsidiary**; but beware if the adverb might be mistaken for an adjective: **A little used** car is not necessarily the same as **a little-used car**, nor a **hard working man** as a **hard-working man**, nor a **pickled onion seller** as a **pickled-onion seller**.

Occasionally a second hyphen may be considered: **an ex-prime minister** suggests a minister past his prime; an **ex-prime-minister** is clear in its meaning but ugly: a better solution would be **former prime minister**.

The hyphen can be omitted from words beginning with **re** and **pre**, except where another **e** follows: **re-entry, pre-empt** but **reopen, preconceive**. Also after **co** except where another **o** follows: **co-ordination** but **coaxial**.

Fractions take hyphens when written out: **two-thirds, one-fifth**. Compass points are hyphenated: **north-east, south-south-west**.

FT style puts hyphens in the following words:

aero-engine	build-up	co-operate
aide-de-camp	bull's-eye	co-ordinate
anti-aircraft	buy-out	D-Ram
attorney-general	by-election	D2-Mac
blow-out	call-up	D-Mark
book-keeper	check-up	director-general
brother-in-law	commander-in-chief	drawing-board

foot-and-mouth disease	pre-Christian	three-fifths *and other fractions*
gilt-edged	pre-eminent	
high-tech	president-elect	three-year-old *horse*
jump-jet	pull-out	timber-framed house
lay-off *noun*	re-election	time-bomb
mother-in-law	re-emerge	turning-point
multi-party	round-up	vice-president
neo-Nazi	running-mate	write-down *noun*
no-man's-land	second-in-command	X-ray
non-combatant	secretary-general	
non-existent	semi-detached	
non-payment	set-up	
north-east *and other compass points*	shake-up	
	think-tank	
	a three-bedroom house	

FT style puts no hyphens in:

agrochemical	eyewitness	lossmaking
aircooled	figleaf	machinegun
airfield	fivefold	marketmaker
antitrust	fundraiser	midweek
biannual	glassmaker	multinational
biennial	gunboat	neoclassical
bondholder	halfhearted	nevertheless
bookbinder	handgun	nonaligned
bylaw	handout	nonconformist
bypass	handover *noun*	nonetheless
byproduct	handpicked	nonplussed
carmaker	hardline	nonstop
carworker	healthcare	offshore
ceasefire	holdup	oilfield
chipmaker	hothead	onshore
coalminer	housebuilder	opencast
coastguard	infrared	overrate
coeducational	interconnect	override
comeback	knowhow	overrule
commonsense *adjective*	lacklustre	peacekeeping
	layout	peacemaker
diehard	leftwing *adjective*	petrochemical
earthmoving	loophole	policymaker

postgraduate
postmortem
postscript
postwar
precondition
prenatal
prewar
profitmaker
rainforest
rearrange
rebirth
reopen
repurchase
restructure
rightwing *adjective*
seabed

semiconductor
shipbuilder
slowdown
soyabean
spinoff
stakeholder
steelmaker
steelworker
strongman
subcommittee
subcontinent
subcontract
subeditor
subhuman
submachinegun
superpower

takeover *noun*
taskforce
teargas
timeshare
toehold
truckmaker
turnround *noun*
underrate
undersecretary
videocassette
videodisc
wartime
widebody *aircraft*
withhold
workforce
worldwide

The following are separate words:

air force
assistant secretary
balance of payments difficulties
capital gains tax
district attorney
general secretary
light year
lord lieutenant
men's wear
on to

orange juice futures
place name
public sector borrowing
    requirement
stock market
take over *verb*
under way
value added tax
vice versa

I

-**ible** among the words that are sometimes misspelt (usually -**able**) are **accessible, admissible, imperceptible, incorruptible, indefensible, inexhaustible, irresistible, permissible, resistible, reversible**.

impact is an overused word; **effect** and **influence** are possible alternatives.

imply is to suggest or insinuate; **infer** is to deduce or conclude.

imposter not -**or**.

imprimatur is approval for a book to be published or for something to be printed. Do not use as a synonym for approval.

index has two plurals: **indexes** for books; **indices** for indicators, numbers. A guide to FT indices is on pages 221–224.

Indonesian names **Mr Rachmat Saleh** first, then **Mr Saleh**. Some Indonesians have one name only: **Mr Suharto**. Remember this and save yourself a lot of time probing the database or annoying the editorial researchers.

initials in the names of people or companies take full points and there should be a space before the surname but not between two initials, thus: **Mr V.P. Singh**.
Company names must include points in their initials: **W.H. Smith**, not **WHSmith**, which is a logo. Note particularly **J.P. Morgan**.

innuendoes is the plural of innuendo.

inquire, **inquiry** are preferred to **enquire, enquiry**.

install has two l's, **instalment** one.

instil has one l, **instilling** two.

intifada The **intifada** (lower case, not italicised) is an uprising, but specifically the Palestinian uprising against Israeli rule in the occupied territories of the Gaza Strip and the West Bank of the Jordan which began in December 1987.

investigations are carried out **of** rather than **into** something.

involve/involved are easily overused, and can often be omitted, especially where no entanglement is at issue.

Irish Republic at first mention, then the **Republic of Ireland**; never **Eire**. Northern Ireland can also be called **Ulster** or sometimes **the province**.

IRA is acceptable in all references to the Irish Republican Army.

Islam is the religion of Moslems, with the **Koran** as its sacred scripture. Mohammed is its chief prophet. **Islamise** (not **Islamicise**) means to convert to Islam or subject to its influence.

issue **Subject**, **topic**, **dispute** are possible alternatives to this overworked word.

it is and there is

"....even Stigand, the patriotic archbishop of Canterbury, found it advisable...."

"Found what?" said the Duck.

"Found it," the Mouse replied rather crossly: "of course you know what 'it' means."

"I know what 'it' means well enough, when I find a thing," said the Duck: "it's generally a frog or a worm. The question is, what did the archbishop find?" (*Alice in Wonderland*)

However, even Lewis Carroll used the construction: "There was a table set out under a tree."

But avoid **it is** and **there is** if possible in a news story.

italics should be used for titles of books, films, plays, operas, ballets, named musical works, computer software packages and television programmes. Titles of paintings, sculptures, etc, are in roman type within quotation marks, as are the names of songs. Titles of newspapers are also in roman.

Italics are used for court cases: *Gutbucket v Cocklecarrot*.

75

Italics are also used sparingly for foreign words and phrases (unless they have been anglicised):

amour propre	*ancien régime*	*chef d'oeuvre*
ex cathedra	*mise en scène*	*nobless oblige*

But most of these could be replaced by English equivalents anyway.

An increasing number of foreign words and phrases have passed into the language and should be printed in roman, even though some contain accents:

ad hoc	doyen	melange
ad nauseam	dramatis personae	menage
aide-de-camp	elite	naive
apropos	émigré	perestroika
attaché	en masse	precis
au gratin	en passant	pro forma
avant garde	esprit de corps	putsch
bete noire	ex officio	rapprochement
blitzkrieg	fait accompli	regime
bona fide	fatwa	résumé
café	gendarme	retroussé
canard	glasnost	rococo
chargé d'affaires	habeas corpus	sine qua non
chateau	hors d'oeuvres	soupçon
chiaroscuro	imprimatur	status quo
cliché	in camera	table d'hote
communiqué	ingenue	tete-a-tete
contretemps	intifada	via
creche	jihad	vice versa
debacle	laisser faire	vis-a-vis
debutante	lèse-majesté	volte-face
décolleté	matinee	

When in doubt use roman. Do not use a foreign word or phrase just to show how clever you are.

Foreign proper nouns should be in roman type: **Academie française, Bundesbank, Land** (German state), **Länder**.

See also **accents**; **drink**; **food**; **foreign words**.

J

jail is preferred to **gaol**.

Jakarta in Java is the capital of Indonesia.

Jane's guides to defence, aircraft, etc; note the apostrophe.

jargon

"Ours is the age of substitutes: instead of language we have jargon; instead of principles, slogans; and, instead of genuine ideas, Bright Ideas."

(Eric Bentley in *New Republic*, 1952.)

"Political language – and with variations this is true of all political parties, from Conservatives to Anarchists – is designed to make lies sound truthful and murder respectable, and to give an appearance of solidity to pure wind."

(George Orwell, *Shooting an Elephant*, 1950.)

Jargon is the language of a particular group or class foisted on to the language as a whole. Its source may be the government (civil service, politicians, military strategists), trade unions, advertising, broadcasting, commerce, computing, industry, medicine, science, popular music or sport; or anyone else who wants to put a cosmetic gloss on their activities or cloak them in language that the average reader finds hard to understand.

Hundreds of jargon words are in daily use already:

accommodation	climate	global
accountability	congruence	globalisation
ambience	core business	hardware
amenities	empathy	implementation
analogous	end product	imprimatur
blueprint	escalate	in-car *entertainment*
burgeoning	exponential	in-house
catalyst	front-end	interface
charismatic	game plan	kick-start

materialise	protagonist	symbiosis
meaningful	rationalisation	target
ongoing	realistic	transportation
optimum	remuneration	unbundling
participation	repositioning	user friendly
phobia	schizophrenic	utilisation
prestigious	software	viable
proliferation	spectrum	

It is important not to fall into the traps set by special interest groups; not to use the language of official contracts, of insurance policies, of computer salespeople or of trade union officials. If we use their jargon we accept their own valuation of themselves, and we will also sometimes be writing incomprehensible copy.

All parts of the FT should be intelligible to all the paper's readers, over two-fifths of whom live outside the UK. Use technical terms in their correct context if you need to, but explain what they mean; avoid the temptation to transfer them out of context: that is what has happened to many of the words listed above.

A selection from newspapers in 1991–93:

As Flyme Airways have found, the people-intensity of a service makes its quality far harder to sustain than that of a product.

At a deeper level, printmaking's Manichean nature was the visual correlation of the Nietzschean antitheses which marked the Expressionist outlook.

Manager G. Grey has to take less of a bottom-up approach and concentrate instead on asset allocation.

Curated by American scholar Violet Rose Green, the Grey show....

Significantly in an industry where three leading players have closed down, ...

For Brown's reductionist verismo, though, substitute Green's accretive rococo...

From an FT press release:

The increasing globalisation of business, the impending single European market in 1992, the necessity to manage rapid technological change, and the emphasis on managerial skills needed to prosper in a recession have radically changed the business environment in the last few years.

This probably changed the environment of the reader, too, who is by now fast asleep.

And from a Brighton Borough Council statement:

All the players in the local economy recognise that the prognosis is bleak, that complacency is unwarranted, and that greater, more proactive public sector leverage is required if Brighton and Hove....are to realise the area's economic potential.

Remember that the man who was studying the frequency distribution of feathered aerofoils in a hostile environment was actually shooting ducks.

Jeddah is a port in Saudi Arabia, sometimes spelt **Jidda** or **Jedda**, but not in the FT.

jew applies to men and women; do not write **jewess**.

jewellery is English, **jewelry** American.

jihad A jihad (roman type, lower case) is a holy war against infidels undertaken by Moslems. **Islamic Jihad** is a pro-Iranian revolutionary group in Lebanon.

Joneses is the plural of someone called **Jones**.

judgment is preferred to **judgement**.

jumbo jet is generally regarded as referring only to the Boeing 747 wide-bodied airliner.

K

Kaffirs are South African gold mining shares.

Kathmandu is the capital of Nepal.

Kazakhstan is a former Soviet republic in central Asia.

kerosene is another name for paraffin when used in aircraft fuel.

key is much overused, especially as a qualifier of decisions, people in industry, etc. **Low key** is especially to be avoided. A fine will be imposed on anyone writing **key player**.

Khartoum is the capital of Sudan.

Khmer is a Cambodian; the **Khmer Rouge** is the Cambodian Communist party; do not, therefore, abbreviate Khmer Rouge to Khmer.

Khrushchev, **Nikita** (1894–1971), former Soviet leader.

kibbutz is an Israeli co-operative settlement; plural **kibbutzim**.

kick-start is what you do to motorcycles, preferably not to economies.

Kilimanjaro in Tanzania is Africa's highest mountain; do not write Mount Kilimanjaro, it is tautologous.

King's Cross in London has an apostrophe; so does **King's Road** in Chelsea, but not all Kings Roads.

knights When people are knighted the new style should be used as soon as it has been announced. However, in certain cases it may be better to wait until the next day before using the new title.
  Example: Norman Fowler resigned as a minister and was immediately knighted. To be accurate our story would have said that **Mr Fowler** resigned and would then have called him **Sir Norman** in referring to his

future plans. It would be better to call him **Mr Fowler** throughout the story and use **Sir Norman** on the following day.

knot is a measure of speed not distance; it measures nautical miles an hour.

knowhow is one word.

Koran is the sacred book of **Islam** *qv*, believed to be the infallible word of God dictated to Mohammed.

Korean names A few surnames dominate: **Kim, Park**, etc. The first word is the surname: **Mr Kim Young-sam** (hyphenating the second two names) followed by **Mr Kim**. The advantage of the hyphenation is that it makes clear which is the surname. However, reporters receiving business cards should be wary of names that have been turned round to Anglicise them.

Kortrijk is a town in West Flanders, Belgium; its French name is **Courtrai**.

Kraków is a city in Poland.

krone, plural **kronor**, is the Swedish currency; **krone**, plural **kroner**, is the Danish currency; **krone**, plural **kroner**, is the Norwegian currency. The Finnish currency is the **markka**.

krugerrands (small **k**) are gold coins issued by the Republic of South Africa.

Ku Klux Klan is a secret organisation of white Protestant Americans, who use violence against minority groups in defence of white supremacy.

Kuomintang is the Taiwanese nationalist political party; since **tang** means party, write **Kuomintang** only.

Kurile Islands are Russian-occupied islands whose ownership is claimed by Japan. The Japanese call them the **Northern Territories**.

KwaNdebele is a South African "homeland".

KwaZulu is a South African "homeland" for Zulus.

Kyrgyzstan is a former Soviet republic in central Asia; this spelling is preferred for the sake of consistency to the (admittedly simpler) Kirghizia.

L

lacunae is the plural of **lacuna**.

laisser faire is a doctrine of unrestricted freedom, non-interference; prefer this spelling to **laissez faire**.

Land (roman not italics, capital L) is a German state, plural **Länder**.

Land's End in Cornwall has an apostrophe.

last and past Be careful when referring to time past. **The last issue of Newsweek** suggests it has closed. **Last week's issue** or **the current issue** or **the latest issue** or **the August issue** are clearer. Note also that in 1994 **last year** is 1993, while **the past year** is the 12 months up to the time of writing. If **last year** means a company's financial year this should be made clear; in some financial stories the context will make this obvious.

late Use **the late** only for people who have died recently, not for those who have been dead a long time.

lawyers *see* **courts**.

lay, lie You **lay** a cover on a bed but **lie** in bed in the morning. To **overlay** is to superimpose, to **overlie** is to rest on.

lay-offs are temporary; **redundancies** or **dismissals** are permanent.

leaflet is a noun not a verb.

Lebanon is the name of the country, not **the Lebanon**.

left, right, and **leftwing, rightwing** as adjectives are lower case. **Leftist, rightist** should be avoided. **Centrist** is permitted for want of a suitable alternative.

legionnaires' disease is a severe form of pneumonia. The name is derived from an outbreak at an American Legion convention in a Philadelphia hotel in July 1976.

lend is a verb, **loan** is a noun (and a verb in the US).

Leningrad in Russia is now again called **St Petersburg**.

less *see* **fewer**.

leukaemia not **leukemia**, which is the American spelling.

Leuven is a town in Brabant, Belgium, French name **Louvain**.

level playing field is a cliché and should be avoided.

libel A guide to the libel laws is on pages 189–192.

librettos is the plural of **libretto**.

licence is a noun, to **license** is a verb.

lift truck is the correct name for what used to be called a **forklift truck**.

likable not **likeable**.

linchpin not **lynchpin**.

liqueur is a flavoured sweetened spirit; **liquor** is any alcoholic drink.

literally should not be used to reinforce a metaphorical exaggeration.

literary references a subject for debate. Two examples:

> **Holly Golightly, you will remember, took herself off to Tiffanys whenever the mean reds hit her. For me N. Bloom & Son, the jewellers has played much the same role...**

> **Before William Boot, newly appointed foreign correspondent of the Daily Beast, set off on assignment to a distant corner of Africa, he made his way to a London outfitter and ordered what he believed to be tools vital to his trade – a dozen cleft sticks with which native runners could carry his despatches to the outside world.**

Do we – does the reader – remember that Holly Golightly was the principal character in Truman Capote's *Breakfast at Tiffany's*? And while William Boot is held in great affection by journalists, is he familiar enough to pass unexplained to the FT's readers, or to whatever readers a publication is aimed towards?

Most people might reasonably be expected to recognise references to, say, Mr Micawber, and to know what is meant by Falstaffian behaviour or Pooterism.

But opinion on the amount of explanation needed will be divided – as it was when the above examples were shown to a cross-section of FT journalists.

Therefore judge your market; remember that the need for explanation may be less in Weekend FT, say, than in a leader page feature. Ask yourself whether understanding the literary reference is essential to appreciation of the story – probably it is not in the examples quoted.

Subs, in particular, should balance the need for adding an explanation against the inevitable interruption to the flow of the copy.

Livorno is a port in Tuscany, Italy; its English name was **Leghorn**, but this can now reasonably be abandoned. **Leghorn** is, however, a breed of chicken.

Lloyd's of London is the insurance market, supported by **Names**, individuals who commit their personal wealth to the market; **Lloyd's List** is the daily newspaper produced by Lloyd's. **Lloyds** is the bank.

loaned is an American form of the word **lent**.

loath is reluctant and is preferred to **loth**; **loathe** is to hate.

locate Try **find**; **location** try **place**.

Lomé is the capital of Togo.

Longchamp is a racecourse in France.

Lord's is the cricket ground in London.

lorry has given way to **truck**.

Loyalist *see* **bias**.

Luxembourg not **Luxemburg**

Lviv is a city in Ukraine; avoid the spellings **Lvov** or **L'vov**.

Lyons is a city in France; we retain the **s**.

M

Macao is an overseas territory of Portugal, on the coast of China, west of Hong Kong. Portuguese spelling is **Macau**.

machinegun, **submachinegun** have no hyphens.

macro-, **micro-** are overused and can often be replaced by large or small.

Madagascar is an island republic of the east coast of Africa; the people are **Malagasy**.

magazine titles should be in roman type, not in quotes.

Magdalen is a college at Oxford University; **Magdalene** a college at Cambridge.

Maghreb countries of north-west Africa include Morocco, Algeria, Tunisia and sometimes Libya.

magistrates' court has an apostrophe.

Maharashtra is a state in India.

major is a military rank but a much overused word in any other context.

Majorca is preferred to **Mallorca**.

Malaysian names It is necessary to know what the surname is: **Dr Mahathir Mohammad** (a medical doctor) becomes **Dr Mahathir** at subsequent references.
  Names of Chinese in Malaysia follow Chinese practice: **Mr Goh Chok Tong**, followed by **Mr Goh** at later references.

manifestos is the plural of **manifesto**.

mankind *see* **bias**.

manoeuvre, **manoeuvring** are often misspelt.

marathon is a race; think carefully before using it to refer to, say, a long negotiating session.

Mareva injunction is a court order freezing someone's assets, usually to prevent a party to arbitration disposing of funds before an award is made.

marginal is often used where **small** would do just as well. Its proper use is as an economic term or analogy in which a small change is highly significant.

marketmaker has no hyphen.

Marseilles is a city in France; French spelling is **Marseille**. The soccer club is called **Olympique Marseille**.

Massachusetts is a US state; note the spelling.

materialise is often used where **happen**, **take place**, **occur** might be sufficient.

matrices is the plural of **matrix**.

Mauritania is a country in West Africa; **Mauretania** is an ancient region of north Africa, now forming parts of Algeria and Morocco.

maxima is the plural of **maximum**.

McDonald's is the fast food chain.

meaningful is too often used to give spurious authority to a story. Try to avoid.

measures This is a mess. No one who has lived long in Britain will be surprised that the country started to embrace metrication enthusiastically and then decided that it was rather vulgar and it would be a terrible pity to lose the mile and the gallon, and anyway why should those foreigners foist their system on us even if it is easier to understand and just look what happened to prices when decimal coinage was introduced, they all went up – and so on.

The result is that children are taught to use metres instead of yards, while signposts throughout the country are still shown in miles. They are taught about litres and millilitres but still order pints in the pub.

The FT finds itself in a similar predicament: some bits are metric, others are rooted in the imperial era. In addition the paper has to cater for three different markets: the UK (partly metric), the Continent of Europe and many other countries (wholly metric) and the US (wholly imperial). This presents particular difficulties for the International Edition.

We therefore have to work to a compromise, but with the general aim of moving away from imperial towards metric.

Weights and measures Custom and practice at the FT is to use the system of units employed in the country being written about. Thus **miles** or **acres** will be used in stories about the UK and the US, whereas **kilometres** or **hectares** will be used for the EC and other countries, including Australia. Put a conversion in parentheses if you think the story will be incomprehensible without one, but bear in mind that most people have a rough idea of what a mile and a kilometre are.

Note that petrol is now measured in litres, not gallons, almost everywhere except in the US.

In technical stories, the style appropriate to the industry should take precedence. Where a rough indicator of distance is required the London paper should use miles, the International Edition kilometres: **Baku is at least 1,000 miles/1,600km from Moscow.** Compromise is inevitable since some London edition pages are unchanged in the International Edition.

Lists of weights and measures and their equivalents in the two systems can be found in the *Concise Oxford Dictionary* and in *Whitaker's Almanack*. The most commonly used are listed in the reference section on pages 193–197.

Mechelen is a city in Belgium; the French name is **Malines**.

Medellín is a town in Colombia.

media, meaning the press and broadcasting, are plural; **mediums** are spiritualists.

medical terms such as **schizophrenic, paralytic** should *never* be used metaphorically.

Medicare is the US health insurance for people aged 65 and above. **Medicaid** is a federal-state scheme that pays for healthcare for low-income families and the disabled.

medieval not **mediaeval**.

meet People meet each other; they do not meet with each other.

men's wear not, definitely not, **menswear**.

Mercosur is the Spanish spelling of a four-nation South American trade pact; Mercosur is preferred to the Portuguese Mercosul.

microchip can usually be shortened to **chip** after first mention.

Mideast for Middle East is acceptable in single-column headlines

Middlesbrough, Cleveland, has only one **o**.

Midwest of the US.

military ranks Military ranks should have initial capitals when used as personal titles, while job titles should be lower case: **Field Marshal Sir John Smith, chief of the general staff (Sir John** at later references); **Colonel Muammer Gadaffi, the Libyan leader** (then **Col Gadaffi**).

Army

Rank	*Abbreviation*
General	Gen
Lieutenant General	Lt Gen
Major General	Maj Gen
Brigadier	Brig
Colonel	Col
Lieutenant Colonel	Lt Col
Major	Maj
Captain	Capt
Lieutenant	Lt
2nd Lieutenant	2nd Lt
Regimental Sergeant Major	RSM
Warrant Officer	WO
Company Sergeant Major	CSM
Sergeant	Sgt
Corporal	Cpl
Lance Corporal	L Cpl
Private	Pte

Navy

Lieutenant Commander	Lt Cmdr
Sub Lieutenant	Sub Lt

Admiral, Commodore, Captain, Commander should not be abbreviated.

Air force

Group Captain	Group Capt
Wing Commander	Wing Cmdr
Squadron Leader	Sqn Ldr
Flight Lieutenant	Flight Lt
Flight Sergeant	Flight Sgt
Leading Aircraftman	LAC

Air Chief/Vice Marshal, Flying Officer, Pilot Officer should not be abbreviated.

militate against is to be detrimental to; **mitigate** is to moderate, make less severe, assuage.

millennium, millennia are often misspelt.

minima is the plural of **minimum**.

ministries are lower case unless the precise title is being used: the (UK) **Department of the Environment** but the **environment department**; **the German justice ministry**

Minorca is preferred to the alternative **Menorca**.

minuscule is often wrongly spelt **miniscule**.

Miss, Mrs, Ms *see* **bias**.

miss out has a dimension not entirely covered by the word **miss**. But try not to overuse the phrase.

Mitterrand has two **t**'s and two **r**'s.

Moldova is a former Soviet republic; this spelling is preferred to **Moldavia**.

Moody's is the US credit rating agency.

moratoriums is the plural of **moratorium**.

Moslem is FT spelling, not **Muslim**.

move can often be replaced by **deal, bid, decision**, etc. **Move** is a useful headline word; beware of overuse.

mpg, mph are acceptable abbreviations for **miles per gallon, miles per hour**.

MPs Normal style is **Mr Tom Brown, Conservative/Labour MP for Anytown;** in the International Edition the member's constituency can be omitted.

There is no need to spell out **member of parliament** unless there is a risk of confusion (with military police, for example).

MS-Dos is Microsoft's personal computer operating system. Note the spelling: FT practice takes precedence over the industry standard. Note also: **CD-Rom, D-Ram, E-Prom, Ram, Rom, S-Ram.**
A glossary of computing terms is on pages 152–157.

Mujahideen are Iranian and Afghan Islamic guerrillas.

Murphy's Law says that if anything can go wrong it will; this applies especially to the Crossword.

music Opera titles, ballets, oratorios and other named musical works should be printed in italics: Verdi's *Un ballo in maschera*, Tchaikovsky's *Swan Lake*, Bach's *St Matthew Passion*, Finzi's *Dies Natalis*, Janáček's *Glagolitic Mass*, Mahler's *Resurrection Symphony* or Mahler's *Symphony No.2*, Schumann's *Dichterliebe*, Strauss's *Alpine Symphony*.

Other works are in roman type with initial capitals: Schubert's Fifth Symphony, Elgar's Violin Concerto, Verdi's Requiem, Beethoven's string quartets.

Titles of cantatas, songs, arias and names of tunes are in roman type within quotes, and follow the capitalisation used in the language of the title: Schubert's "Die Taubenpost", Brahms's "Von ewiger Liebe", Mahler's "Ich bin der Welt abhanden gekommen", "Ella giammai m'amo" from *Don Carlos*, Cole Porter's "Begin the Beguine".

Most other musical terms should be in roman type: allegro, andante, crescendo, obbligato, scherzo, trio; they should have an initial capital only where they are the title of a movement: the Adagio from Mahler's Fifth Symphony. Little known words and phrases should be in italics: "...the blend of *dolcezza* and *cantabile* in the finale".

Note that Lieder has a capital L.

Record, CD and tape album titles should be in italics.

myriad means a large number and should not be followed by of: a **myriad schemes** is correct, not **a myriad of schemes**. Use with caution.

N

N-weapons, **N-arms**, etc, are to be discouraged; try always to use the word **nuclear** instead, even in headlines.

Nagorno-Karabakh, formerly an administrative division of the Soviet Union, has been the subject of a war between Armenia and Azerbaijan, a dispute which was won by Armenia.

naivety not naiveté or naïveté.

Name A Lloyd's Name supports the Lloyd's of London insurance market by pledging his or her personal wealth.

names and titles First names should always be given. People are called Mr, Mrs, Ms, Miss, Lord, Lt Gen as appropriate in the news and features sections of the FT.

However, Mr, Mrs, etc, are not used in:

The front page summary column
Headings
Captions
Weekend FT
Arts and Books pages
Observer column
Management page
Technology page
Environment page

or for: **people in show business, sportsmen** and **the dead**.

In general the name comes before the title: **Mr John Major, the British prime minister** followed by **Mr Major** in all later references; never **prime minister Major, chancellor Kohl**. **US president Bill Clinton** becomes **Mr Clinton** on second mention. If the person referred to is little known, the title can be placed first: **The head of the Libyan armed forces, General Abu Bakr Yunis Jaher**.

Initials take full points and there should be a space before the surname but not between two initials: **Mr V.P. Singh**.

Company names must include points in their initials: **W.H. Smith**, not **WHSmith**, which is what appears above the shops.

In captions full names should be given, omitting Mr, Ms, etc; examples:

Jaques Delors faces the cameras after yesterday's meeting
or
Sir Leon Brittan: determined to remove barriers

See also **capitals**; **doctors**.

Nanjing, also spelt **Nan-ching or Nanking**, is a city in eastern China.

naphtha People are often fooled by the **phth** in the middle.

Nato can be used in all references to the North Atlantic Treaty Organisation.

navy ranks *see* **military names**.

nebulas is the plural of **nebula**.

Netherlands is the country; **Holland** is two of its provinces (North Holland, South Holland).

new age, a 1980s philosophy, is characterised by a belief in alternative medicine, astrology, spiritualism, meditation, etc.

new year is lower case, but note **New Year's day/eve**.

Newcastle-under-Lyme is in Staffordshire; **Newcastle upon Tyne** (no hyphens) is in north-east England.

newspaper titles are printed in roman type without quotes, not in italics. The word **the** sometimes forms part of the title: **The Times** but **the Financial Times**.

When referring to what the Daily Telegraph used to call "another newspaper", give its title.

nevertheless is one word.

nicknames or abbreviated names can be used where someone is always known by one: **Mr Tiny Rowland**; **Mr Tony Benn**.

Nippon Never use this as an abbreviation for any of the hundreds of Japanese companies which have Nippon as part of their name.

no one is preferable to **nobody**.

no-man's-land Note hyphens and apostrophe.

Nobel Prize has initial capitals: **Nobel Peace Prize**. They are awarded for chemistry, literature, peace, physics and physiology or medicine. The Nobel Memorial Prize in Economic Science was established by the Swedish central bank as a memorial to Alfred Nobel.

non- words are not usually hyphenated: **nonaligned**, **nonconformist**, **nonplussed**, **nonstop**.

nonetheless is one word.

North Rhine Westphalia is a German state; the German name is **Nordrhein-Westfalen**.

Northern Ireland can also be called **Ulster**, or occasionally **the province**. Historically Ulster includes two counties now in the Irish Republic.

nuclear energy A glossary of terms is on pages 198–199.

numbers *see* **figures**.

Nuremberg is a city in southern Germany; the German name is **Nürnberg**.

O

obscenities *see* **expletives**.

obsolescent means becoming **obsolete** or out of date.

occur, **occurred**.

offshore, **onshore** have no hyphens.

oilfield has no hyphen.

Olympiad has come to refer to the staging of the modern Olympic Games; strictly it means the four-year period between consecutive games. Originally it was a unit of Greek chronology.

on to not **onto**.

ongoing is a vile word.

only should be as close as possible to the words it qualifies: **Virgin, which only won its licence for the route in June**, suggests that in June the airline did nothing else. ...**which won the right....only in June** is correct.
   Similarly, after reading that *in* **Turkey, children can only watch TV commercials in the presence of an adult**, one might wonder why they are not allowed to watch anything else with an adult present.

opera titles are printed in italics. Normal practice is to spell the name of an opera in the language in which it is being sung in a particular production. Thus at the Royal Opera House, Covent Garden you might expect to see *Il Barbiere di Siviglia*; at the English National Opera *The Barber of Seville*.

Some difficult and accented spellings:

Il Barbiere di Siviglia	Rossini
Béatrice et Bénédict	Berlioz
La Bohème	Puccini

Così fan tutte	Mozart, *note lower case*
Die Dreigroschenoper	Weill
Die Entführung aus dem Serail	Mozart
Der fliegende Holländer	Wagner
Die Frau ohne Schatten	Richard Strauss
Der Freischütz	Weber
Gianni Schicchi	Puccini
Götterdämmerung	Wagner
Hänsel und Gretel	Humperdinck
L'Incoronazione di Poppaea	Monteverdi
Katya Kabanova	Janácek
Lakmé	Delibes
Die lustigen Weiber von Windsor	Nicolai
Die Meistersinger von Nürnberg	Wagner
Le Nozze di Figaro	Mozart
Les Pêcheurs des Perles	Bizet
Pelléas et Mélisande	Debussy
Samson et Dalila	Saint-Saëns
Tannhäuser	Wagner
La traviata	Verdi
Il trovatore	Verdi
Die Walküre	Wagner
Die Zauberflöte	Mozart

ophthalmic Another word with **phth** in the middle.

opinion polls Always say who carried out the poll and for whom; remember that Gallup is a trade name.

optimum should not be used as a synonym for best.

oral agreement is a spoken one; any agreement is verbal whether spoken or written because it uses words.

oratorios is the plural of **oratorio**.

ordinance is an authoritative regulation or decree; **ordnance** is artillery, military supplies or munitions.

organisations and groupings A list of organisations is on pages 200–211.

orient (verb) is a variant of **orientate**; prefer the latter.

Orkney Islands or **Orkney**, islands off the north-east of Scotland; do not write **Orkneys**.

Ostend, Belgian port, not **Oostende** or **Ostende**.

Ouagadougou is the capital of Burkina Faso, formerly Upper Volta.

ouster is a legal term for the act of eviction from property; in any other sense (such as removal as the head of a political party) the word to use is **ousting**; or **overthrow**.

over Do not write **over the year** if you mean **during the year**. A phrase such as **just over 1,000 litres** is quite acceptable and should not be changed to **just more than**...

overall appears in the FT roughly 100 times a week. Often it is meaningless; sometimes it can be replaced by **average** or **total** or **aggregate**.

Oxbridge should be avoided as a synonym for Oxford and Cambridge.

oxymoron is a figure of speech in which contradictory terms are used in conjunction. Dictionary examples are **cruel kindness**, **falsely true**, while Shakespeare in *Romeo and Juliet* referred to **loving hate**. However, the examples below, drawn from the national newspaper database, show that the term has been used by journalists to indulge some prejudices:

boxing ethics	literary event
British management	loyal rightwinger
cautious aggression	merry Christmas
colourful accountant	military intelligence
English cuisine	official nickname
English justice	open secret
focused conglomerate	pleasant villain
French queue	poor bookmaker
friendly fire	public transport
great economist	publishing management
jumbo prawns	vegetarian haggis
kindly malice	warm salad
legitimate crime	

P

paediatrics is the branch of medical science dealing with children.

paintings and the titles of other works of art are in roman type within quotes.

Papua New Guinea, islands in the south-west Pacific, has no hyphens.

parentheses *see* **brackets**.

Paris Club is a group of industrial countries which meets regularly in Paris to discuss debt rescheduling of debtor countries with payments difficulties.

Parkinson's Law states that work expands to fill the time allotted to it. Author: C. Northcote Parkinson.

parliament, **parliamentary** are always lower case except when referring to the Houses of Parliament as a building.

If you use the name of a foreign parliament, explain what it is: **the Folketing, the Danish parliament; the Bundestag, the lower house of the German parliament**. Others are the **Althing** (Iceland), **Dáil** (Ireland), **Diet** (Japan), **Knesset** (Israel), **Riksdag** (Sweden), **Storting** (Norway). But it is usually sufficient to refer, for example, to the **Icelandic parliament**.

In the US, **Congress** consists of the Senate and the House of Representatives. Members are **senators** or **congressmen**.

partially means incomplete, to a limited degree; **partly** means to some extent.

party is lower case (**the Labour party**) when it is the last word of the title, but has a capital otherwise: **Party of Hope**.

past *see* **last**.

peers Use the previous name until a newly created peer has chosen a title: **Mr Bloggs, who was given a life peerage in the new year honours list**. All peers below the rank of duke – marquesses, earls, viscounts and barons – are called Lord So-and-so. Those who have a place name in their title will be given it only in parliamentary reports unless there are two with the same name. Women life peers should be referred to as life peers, not peeresses.

A duke should be referred to as the **Duke of Plazatoro**; subsequent references **the duke**.

peninsula is a noun, **peninsular** an adjective.

Pep is a **personal equity plan**.

per annum, **per capita** Preferably write **a year, a head**.

per cent is written out in text, % in heads.

Remember that a rise in the mortgage rate from 11 per cent to 12 per cent is not a 1 per cent rise but a **1 percentage point rise** or a **1 point rise**. It is important to get this right. Failure to do so is a barrier to promotion.

persons are generally **people**, which is preferred use.

perspicacity is acute perception, discernment; **perspicuity** is being lucid, easily understood.

persuade does not mean **convince**. People are persuaded to do something but convinced of the wisdom of doing so.

Peter Principle states that every member of a hierarchy is promoted to his (or her) own level of incompetence. Authors: Lawrence J. Peter and Raymond Hull.

phenomena is the plural of **phenomenon**.

Philippines The people are **Filipinos**.

Phnom Penh is the capital of Cambodia.

phone (no apostrophe) is acceptable in heads; otherwise write **telephone**.

phoney not **phony**.

phosphorus is a nonmetallic element; **phosphorous** describes a substance containing phosphorus.

places follow *Times Atlas* spelling with a few exceptions.

Plaid Cymru is the Welsh nationalist party.

plane is used to shave wood; what you fly in is an **aircraft, jet, airliner, helicopter**, etc. *See* **aircraft names**.

planets and other heavenly bodies should have initial capitals: **Alpha Centauri, Halley's comet, Mars, Sirius, Venus**.

The planet earth, the sun and the moon should have initial capitals when listed with other heavenly bodies, but not when on their own.

plateaux is the plural of **plateau**.

play titles should be printed in italics with initial capitals for words other than conjunctions, articles and prepositions: *A Man for all Seasons*.

player is a member of a sports team, or a musician, not someone involved in a takeover. **Player** for **participant** trivialises, as does **actor** in the same context.

plc means **public limited company**; it is normally omitted in the FT unless it is necessary to distinguish between a parent company and a subsidiary.

plurals the plural of most words in English is made by adding an **s**; this is quite simple, except where the word ends with an **a** or **eau** or **f** or **o** or **um** or **x** or where it already ends in **s**.

Difficulty in deciding the correct plural arises because many of these words come from Latin and no one learns Latin at school any more. Remember that **media** and **data** remain plural nouns (**the data are**...) in the FT. It is too late to do anything about **agenda**, which is now a singular noun, plural **agendas**.

With compound titles the principal word takes the plural form: **aides-de-camp, attorneys-general, commanders-in-chief, governors-general, presidents-elect, detective sergeants, lord mayors**; note also **courts martial**.

The FT's preferred style leans towards popular usage rather than that used in technical writing (**formulas** not formulae, **antennas** not antennae).

See also **apostrophes**.

101

police ranks

Rank	Abbreviation
Superintendent	Supt
Detective Sergeant	Det Sgt
Inspector	Insp
Police Sergeant	Sgt
Police Constable	PC

Remember to use a neutral form such as **police** or **police officers**, not policemen.

politburo is the executive and policymaking committee of a Communist party.

political correctness often abbreviated to PC, is the persecution of people suspected of having nonconformist thoughts about race and gender. A concept born in American universities, in recent years it has crossed the Atlantic. At its heart it is reaction against a culture that is said to have been shaped by Dwems – dead white european males (Shakespeare etc).

In the language of PC a cowboy becomes a **cowperson**, the bald man is **follicularly challenged**, the short person **vertically challenged**, the old person **chronologically gifted**; the handicapped are **physically challenged** or even **differently abled**; it has even been suggested that the 40-stone man has an **alternative body image**; history should be **herstory** and seminars **ovulars**. A girl becomes a **pre-woman** and a woman a **person of gender**, a remarkable phrase since it fails to tell you in three words what the word it replaces does in one. **Negative patient care outcome** – death – is another fine example.

Treat PC with extreme caution; much of its terminology is absurd. But remember that as a result of the move towards euphemisms old-age pensioners are now **senior citizens**, the crippled are **handicapped**, cars are **pre-used** rather than just secondhand, dustmen are **refuse collectors**, criminals are **offenders** and drug addiction has become **substance abuse**.

Other words have made some progress towards acceptance: **humankind** instead of mankind for example, or **Inuit** for Eskimo. Think carefully before admitting any more.

A guide to FT practice appears under **bias**.

political parties The word **party** is lower case when it is the final word in a title; capitalised elsewhere: the **Conservative party**, the **Social Democratic and Labour party**, the **Party of God**. *See also* **capitals**.

poll tax is acceptable for the discredited **community charge**; its replacement is the **council tax**. In the FT International Edition these taxes must be explained.

Port-au-Prince is the capital of Haiti.

Portuguese and Brazilian names A Mr Tancredo de Almeida Neves is
usually a **Mr Neves** (his father's name), not a **Mr de Almeida** (probably his mother's name). However, practice can vary from family to family and individual to individual.

Some names, especially in Brazil, end with **Filho**, **Neto** or **Sobrinho**; these words start with capital letters in the context but are not names. They mean **son**, **grandson** and **nephew**, respectively. They are used in families rather as US dynasties use Roman numerals, such as John P. Heinz III.

So **Mr Antonio Delfim Neto** is a **Mr Delfim**, not a **Mr Neto**; **Mr João Alves Filho** is a **Mr Alves**, not a **Mr Filho**.

In Brazil the maternal name is sometimes the accepted surname; when in doubt use both.

Note the spelling of the common Portuguese first name **João** (equivalent of John).

Some common names and words

Eletrobrás	Brazilian electricity generator
Pão de Açúcar	Brazilian supermarket chain
" " "	sugar loaf landmark in Rio
Pérez de Cuéllar, Javier	former UN secretary-general
Petrobrás	Brazilian national oil and gas company
São Paulo	Brazilian city
Telebrás	Brazilian telecoms company

position where it means situation can often be avoided; so can **situation**.

post- as a prefix has no hyphens: **postgraduate**, **posthaste**, **postmortem**, **postscript**, **postwar**.

practicable means capable of being effected; **practical** means adapted to actual conditions. The negatives are **impracticable**, **unpractical**.

practice is a noun, **practise** a verb.

pre- as a prefix has no hyphens unless it is followed by a word beginning with e: **pre-empt, precondition, prenatal, prewar**.

precipitate (adjective) means rash or hasty; **precipitous** means very steep.

predictable Beware: it can easily be seen to mean that the writer was clever enough to know in advance: **the Ruritanian-controlled federal government reacted with predictable anger...**

prefixes should be hyphenated if the word that follows is capitalised (**anti-American, anti-Semitic**), or if the word that follow starts with the same vowel (**anti-inflationary, co-ordinate, pre-eminent**). Otherwise do not use a hyphen (**antitrust, decommission, overrate, postwar, precondition, reopen, rerun, semiconductor, subcontinent, submachinegun**). *See also* **hyphens.**

premier should be reserved for heads of provinces and states; it is sometimes used for the prime ministers of smaller countries. Countries generally have prime ministers, though premier may be used in an emergency in a headline.

prepositions There is no need to be pedantic about using a preposition at the end of a sentence. It is obviously unnecessary to rewrite a sentence such as: **He bought every picture he could lay his hands on** so that it ends ... **on which he could lay his hands**. Ben Jonson wrote: "Prepositions follow sometimes the nouns they are coupled with."

If the final preposition sounds comfortable, keep it; if it does not, still keep it unless an alternative is obviously less awkward. Winston Churchill once complained about a sentence that clumsily avoided a prepositional ending: "This is the sort of nonsense up with which I will not put."

Take care when choosing prepositions: **a strike against unfair dismissals** is preferable to a strike **over** them; the **slide of a currency** preferable to the slide **in** it. The constraints of space when writing headlines may allow some relaxation in favour of a shorter word.

Beware of using too many prepositions: **the inflation rate is back up to 6 per cent** would be just as informative if **up** was omitted.

presently means **soon**, not at present; **currently** means **at present**.

presidium not **praesidium**.

press conference phrases such as **told a press conference, told journalists** or even **told the Financial Times** can usually be omitted; **said** is often adequate. It is acceptable to use the FT's name in the context of, say, an exclusive interview with a country's president; but in other cases take care.

press reports Quote a source for press reports if possible, particularly if the reports are likely to be less than impartial.

pressure should not be used as a verb to mean **put pressure on**.

prime minister can be abbreviated to **PM** in heads in the FT's London edition. Beware of doing this on International Edition pages or on London pages that are unchanged in the International Edition. *See also* **premier**.

principal is important, chief (noun or adjective); **principle** means fundamental or general truth (noun). Debt repayments are made of **principal**. Heads of schools are sometimes **principals**.

Princes Street in Edinburgh has no apostrophe.

prior to can always be replaced by **before**, though preferably not by **ahead of**.

privy council is the council of state of a monarch.

probe is a useful word for headlines but others are preferable in text (**inquire, investigate**).

procrastinate is to put off or defer; **prevaricate** is to speak or act falsely.

profits Operating, gross, pretax or net? Be clear about what you mean.

prolife is used, particularly in the US, to refer to organisations and pressure groups opposed to abortion. The term **anti-abortion** should be used in the FT, not **prolife**.

proofreading Important: writers and subeditors should use the system's spelling checker on every story. Subs should always:

(a) Double check a story with the page layout. Ensure that fonts, typesizes and column measures are correct. Much of this is done automatically by the page layout system.

105

(b) Check for bad word breaks and correct them if possible; refer words that break badly to the system dictionary. The dictionary can then be amended.

(c) Soft-typeset the story if you have time, to check for headline fit, widows and orphans.

(d) Double check the cross references; wrong or missing cross references are probably the most common error in the FT.

protagonist is the principal character in a play or story. There cannot be several in one plot.

protest Americans **protest a decision**; in the UK, and especially in the FT, people **protest against** or **at** something; you can, however, protest your innocence. People protesting are **protesters**.

proved is preferred to **proven**, except when writing about the Scottish court verdict **not proven** or about oil and gas reserves.

Pulitzer Prize has initial capitals, but the categories are lower case. The prizes are awarded yearly for American journalism, literature and music.

punctuation *see* **stops**.

Punjab Do not write **the Punjab**.

puns

"On the whole we are hostile to puns"
(Wolcott Gibbs quoted by James Thurber, *The Years with Ross*, 1959)

One day's issues of the British national press in 1992 contained these headline puns:

A clash of symbols
Heinz gives Graf more variety
When brain sells go bust
Hedge against this inflation *about Sissinghurst*
Return of the incredible sulk
Surgeon Pauline, lady of the camps
Barber lacks a cutting edge
Christie's profits hit as art makes a bad impression
Elliott still out on limb *leg injury to athlete*

Hall or nothin' to keep Keegan
Pears so ripe for picking *a footballer*
Pears' work bears fruit *the same footballer*
She's Jess a country girl at heart
It's pay time at thigh-school
Grievous bodily Farm *about a rock group*
Singing meter maid is just the ticket!
My old man just drove me crockers
Walt's dizzy heights of fantasy
Stone me if Mick doesn't love being a grandad *Jagger*
Mutiny in the high Cs
Stephenson rockets in
Yawn of a new era for telly
Johnny's rotten to Jacko
Boklash
Stirring up a mayor's nest
Game for everything *about a cook*
Deals on meals
With fiends like these
In the trap of luxury
Full Marx
Art of darkness
The Wurm that turned
Can the Rothschilds bank on the next generation?
Renault to take the private road
Peek stays at amber *a traffic lights manufacturer*
Graseby reads a £20m print-out *an electronics group*
Hillsdown £11m deal in the can *a food processing group*
O&M takes off with DHL's £14m *an air courier*
Turnip for the books *a restaurant*
GPA ready to take off at last
Cherry Blossom blacking (*The government yesterday took the shine off...*).

Only the first appeared in the FT. The remainder were published on a quiet day for the tabloid sports desks: after the weekend sports fixtures the total would be much higher.

Of these 40 or so examples perhaps half a dozen are witty and original. The remainder appear to have been written because that is what the newspaper expected or because the sub was bored; the items culled from the financial pages (at the bottom of the list) are especially tired.

It is unreasonable to expect all such puns to be banned from the pages of the FT, particularly in features, in Weekend FT and on the Arts page. But think carefully before you commit yourself: is the pun apt? is it funny? is it new?

Q

Quebec The people are **Québecois**.

quango is a quasi-autonomous non-governmental organisation.

Queen, the Prefer **Queen Elizabeth** unless it is absolutely certain who is referred to; **the Queen** at later references. The Queen Mother's full title is **Queen Elizabeth the Queen Mother**. The ship can be called the **QE2** at all references.

Queen's College in Oxford and London; **Queens' College**, Cambridge; **Queen's University**, Belfast.

quorums is the plural of **quorum**.

quotation marks should be used for words, phrases and sentences from a clearly identified source. This applies as much to headlines as to the stories under them.

Quotation marks should not be used in a vain attempt to make slang respectable nor to give a phrase a meaning which it would not ordinarily bear; they should not appear round words in headings unless in the story concerned the words are directly attributed to a speaker. They should not be used in headlines to highlight allegations rather than facts: **Brown a 'murderer'**.

Single quotes should be used in headings; double quotes in text. Single quotes are used for quotes within quotes.

Quotation marks should be placed where they belong: In **Oxford is " the home of lost causes"**. the full point belongs to the sentence as a whole rather than to the words in quotes; it should therefore be placed outside the quotes: **Did Nelson really say "Kiss me Hardy"?**

A composite example:

Mr Green said: "The test of principles is how you put them into effect." He added that Labour's new framework would give the unions "commensurate responsibilities". Mr Albert Hall criticised Labour's changes as deceptions

which did not "amount to a row of beans". Mr Green replied that Mr Hall was obviously "barking mad". He added: "It is obviously time that Mr Hall was locked away."

Note that quoted text starts with a capital letter when it follows a colon.

Avoid the overuse of quotes to report common words. They can be omitted, for example, from: **Mr White said he would "retire from public life" after the election.**

Further examples are given in *Fowler's Modern English Usage* and in *Hart's Rules for Compositors and Readers.*

Titles of paintings, sculptures, poems, songs and arias are in roman type within quotes. Titles of books, films, plays, operas, ballets and computer software packages are in italics with no quotes. *See also* **italics.**

R

R&D is the abbreviation for research and development.

race *see* **bias.**

radii is the plural of radius.

rainforest is one word.

Ras al-Khaimah is a member state of the United Arab Emirates.

ratios Write **21 to 14** rather than **21:14** or **21-14**.

re words should not be hyphenated unless two e's would abut: **rearrange, rebirth, re-entry, re-examine, repurchase**. Exceptions are **re-cover** (meaning cover again), **re-form** (form again).

realistic is sometimes used where **sensible, reasonable, likely, practical** would be better: **The union said it was waiting for a realistic (big?) offer.**

reason To write **the reason for this is because** is unnecessary; **this is because** or **the reason for this is that** is sufficient.

rebut, refute require evidence and mean more than deny or repudiate. **Refute** should not be used when someone merely denies.

recession is a decline in economic activity, defined as two consecutive falls in real gross national product. A **depression** is a prolonged period of low economic activity.

referendums People vote **Yes** or **No** in referendums, initial capitals, no quotes.

register office is where people marry, not **registry**.

religions use an initial capital when writing about a specific body or denomination: **the Church of England, Islam, Jehovah's Witnesses, Plymouth Brethren, Roman Catholic Church** (just **Catholic** at later reference), **Salvation Army, Christian, Buddhist, God, Moslem, Protestant**, etc. The church in a general sense is lower case: **the church's views on poverty, St Mary's church.**

Write **clergy** rather than **clergymen**, since many are women.

Islam is the religion of **Moslems**. Usually **Islamic** refers to the religion, Moslem to people, architecture, politics, etc.

See also **capitals, churchmen.**

renaissance as a style of art, architecture, etc, has a lower case **r**; the **Renaissance** as a period of history has a capital.

reported speech This is important. Errors in reported speech, especially in the sequence of tenses, are still a common source of error in the FT and elsewhere.

In indirect speech the tense of the verb must relate to the tense of the reporting verb. When reporting what someone said, the present tense of direct speech usually becomes past tense in reported speech: **Mr Major said: "I am very pleased with the result of the Danish referendum"** becomes in a news story **Mr Major said he was very happy with the result...**

Confusion may be caused because headlines are always written in the present tense. Remember that while the past and perfect tenses are used in news stories to anchor the events at a particular time (usually the previous day), in scenes and features the sequence of present and perfect tenses may be preferred to remove the events from a specific period of time. Thus when John Major says the words: **"Sterling will not rejoin the ERM in the foreseeable future"** he may be reported as follows:

1. Headline:
Major says sterling will not rejoin ERM.

2. News story text:
Mr Major said yesterday that sterling would not try to re-enter the exchange rate mechanism in the foreseeable future.

3. Feature or news analysis:
Mr Major says (or has said) that sterling will not re-enter the ERM until the conditions are right. He says (or has said) that structural flaws must be corrected before any further moves take place.

One of the most common errors is to write **will** in the second example instead of **would**.

However, make sure the meaning is clear: **He said that his son lived in New York** does not explain whether the son still lives there; a direct quote may be preferable.

If you are in any doubt about the correct use of reported speech, read reports of court cases. Court reporters are trained to be meticulous in this respect.

responsible People can be responsible, things cannot. **The newspaper's price rise was responsible for a drop in readership**. It was not; it caused it.

restaurateur owns or runs a restaurant; beware the rogue **n** that often creeps into this word.

reticent means uncommunicative, taciturn, reserved; **reluctant** means unwilling or disinclined: **Companies are reticent** (should be **reluctant**) **to throw away existing computers**.

Reuters is the news agency; in copy write **Reuter reports**...

Reykjavik is the capital of Iceland.

Rheims is a city in France; this spelling is preferred to **Reims**.

Richter scale is used to measure the force of earthquakes. It ranges from 0 (a man jumping off a table) to 10 (350 hydrogen bombs). The scale is logarithmic: each unit is 10 times larger than the one below it.

right, **left** and **rightwing, leftwing** as adjectives are lower case. **Rightist, leftist** must be avoided. **Centrist** is permitted for want of a suitable alternative. **Conservative** (with a small c) can be considered as an alternative to **rightwing**.

ro-ro is the abbreviation for a roll on-roll off ferry.

Robin Hood's Bay in North Yorkshire; note the spelling.

Romania not **Rumania**.

row is a useful headline word, but be careful not to use it where what has happened is not more than a slight disagreement.

run-up is a hackneyed phrase, especially before elections; **before** is preferable.

Russian names In general Russian names should end in **y** after a consonant and in **i** after a vowel, with one exception: **Yuri** since two **y**'s in a short name look strange.

Hence **Yevgeny, Grigory, Georgy, Anatoly, Dmitry** and **Vasily**, but **Alexei, Andrei** and **Sergei**; **Mr Yavlinsky** but the **Bolshoi** and **General Rutskoi**.

Names should also be spelt phonetically and as simply as possible. For example, with the standard Russian **e** pronounced **ye** we should write **Yegor** and not **Egor**; **Yevgeny** not **Evgeny, Evgenny** or **Eugene**. The fewer characters the better: **Vasily** not **Vassily, Boiko** not **Boycko**.

There are a few exceptions to the phonetic rule: although **Gorbachev** is pronounced **Gorbachov** (this is because the last vowel is a special Russian **e** with Umlaut pronounced something like **io**), we write **Gorbachev** because of tradition and because it makes little difference to how his name is pronounced.

But because the special **e** is the first vowel in the name of the former deputy prime minister, it is important to write **Fyodorov** not **Fedorov** (even though he himself writes it that way on his English language business card) because Fedorov is much more misleading than Gorbachev.

In the few cases where names are also identical to western spelling, bar one character, the western version should be used: **Alexander** not **Alexandr**.

Also beware of ending Russian names with **e** or **ff**, which are French transliterations. It should be **Maxim** not **Maxime**, **Matiukhin** not **Matiukhine**, **Fyodorov** not **Fyodoroff**.

Place names should be spelt as they are internationally known: **Kiev** not **Kiv** or **Kiyev**; **Yekaterinburg** not **Ekaterinburg** or **Yekaterinaburg**.

Endings **-ia** and **-iev** are preferred to **-iya** or **-iyev**: **Izvestia** not **Izvestiya**, **Nabiev** not **Nabiyev**, **Yevgenia** not **Yevgeniya**.

Some common names and words

Bolshoi	Rutskoi
Dnepr *not Dnieper*	Schnittke *not Shnitke*
Gerashchenko *not Gerashenko*	Skryabin *not Scriabin*
Khasbulatov	Tchaikovsky
Khrushchev	Tupolev *not Tupolyev*
Rakhmaninov *not Rachmaninov*	

Rwanda, East African republic, not **Ruanda**.

S

saccharin is a sweetener, **saccharine** the adjective derived from it.

sacrilegious is often wrongly spelt **sacreligious**.

Sadler's Wells was named after a Mr Sadler and has an apostrophe.

said is the best verb to report someone's speech; other verbs may suggest either that the writer agrees with the speaker or does not believe him. Be careful, therefore, with verbs such as **claimed, admitted, alleged, asserted, conceded, emphasised, stressed**.

The words **made clear** are sometimes used precisely to explain opinions that a speaker is unwilling to have directly attributed to him. Subs should check with the writer before changing **made clear** to **said**.

Saint there is little consistency in the spelling of places named after saints. Note the following:

St Albans, Hertforshire
St Andrews, Scotland
St Catharine's College, Cambridge
St Catherine's College, Oxford
St Clement Danes, London
St Helens, Lancashire
St James's Park/Palace, London
Saint John, New Brunswick, Canada
St John's, Antigua, Newfoundland
St John's Wood, London
St Katharine's Dock, London
St Martin-in-the Fields, London
St Petersburg, formerly Leningrad.

Sahara is a desert in North Africa; do not write **Sahara desert**.

saleable not **salable**.

salutary means promoting a beneficial effect; the word **salutory** does not exist.

salvos is the plural of **salvo**.

sanatoriums is the preferred plural of **sanatorium**.

São Paulo is a state and city in Brazil.

São Tomé e Principe is a country in West Africa.

Savile Row in London; note the spelling.

savings and loans (S&Ls) provide funds for house purchase in the US.

Scandinavia is Denmark, Norway and Sweden; **the nordic countries** are these plus Finland and Iceland.

scenario can usually be replaced by **scheme, plan, programme**. It should be reserved for its technical use in **scenario planning**, which means a dramatic representation of what might become the future. This is not the same as a **forecast, expectation** or **prediction**.

schizophrenia should be used only to describe the medical condition. This also applies to other terms such as **geriatric, paralytic, spastic**.

Schleswig-Holstein is a German state.

Scilly Islands lie off the south-west coast of England; write **Scilly Islands** or **Isles of Scilly** but not the **Scillies**.

scotch means put an end to, render harmless; the people are **Scots, Scottish** or **Scotsmen/women**; the eggs, pine trees, whisky and wool are **Scotch**, as is the mist.

seabed, seafront, seashore have no hyphens.

seasons are lower case; **seasonable** is suitable for the time of year; **seasonal** is relating to a particular season. Beware of writing about seasons in the UK as if they apply elsewhere in the world.

seatbelt is one word.

second world war not World War II or any other variant.

see, sees, saw People and animals see, companies and years do not. Avoid: **ICI saw its profits fall** or **1995 is expected to see a new series of laws**.

semicolons *see* **stops**.

Sephardim are Jews of Spanish or Portuguese descent; **Ashkenazim** are German or east European Jews.

Sevastopol is a port and resort in Ukraine; prefer this spelling to the (English) **Sebastopol**.

sewage is the waste matter, **sewerage** the arrangement that deals with it.

Shakespearean is the adjective from Shakespeare.

sheikh not **sheik**.

Sherpas are people of Mongolian origin living in Nepal; but in the FT the word **sherpa** is more likely to refer to a senior official who prepares the ground for international conferences and summit meetings. In this context a lower case **s** is used.

Shetland off the north coast of Scotland; write **Shetland Islands** or **Shetland** but not the **Shetlands**.

Shia Moslems belong to one of the two main branches of orthodox Islam (**Sunni** is the other); write **Shia** not **Shi'ite**.

shippers are usually customers of **shipowners**; do not confuse the two.

ships are neuter not female; their names should be in roman type not italics. The size of ships is usually measured in **gross registered tonnage (grt)**. The size of tankers and dry bulk cargo ships is measured in **deadweight tonnes (dwt)**. Container ships are sometimes measured in **teu (twenty foot equivalent units)**.

A glossary of common shipping terms is on pages 212–213.

Siena is a city in Tuscany; the pigment is **sienna**.

sierra is a mountain range; **Sierra Nevada mountains** is therefore tautologous.

significantly is much overused to give phoney continuity.

silicon is a commonly found element widely used in electronic components, glass, building materials, etc; **silicone** is a synthetic material with good insulating and lubricating properties, used as oils, water-repellents, resins, etc. Do not confuse the two.

Sinn Féin is the Irish republican political movement.

siphon not **syphon**.

situation is much overused and can often be omitted.

sizeable not **sizable**.

Smithsonian Institution, the US group of museums, is so spelt, *not* **Institute**.

song titles are set in roman type within quotes, with principal words capitalised: "Gimme a Pigfoot and a Barrel of Beer". Foreign titles should follow the style used in the relevant language: "Che gelida mannina"; "Dies Bildnis ist bezaubernd schön".

sources Diplomatic sources are **diplomats**; ministerial sources are **ministers**; Whitehall sources are **officials**. Avoid **sources** if possible, especially those often described as reliable or well informed. **Circles** and **observers** are also best avoided. Be as specific as you can about the origin of a story.

Sotheby's, the auction house, has an apostrophe.

souk is a marketplace in eastern Moslem countries; the plural is the same.

soyabean is not hyphenated; **soybean** is the American spelling.

Spanish names A **Mr Jaime Rodríguez Martínez** is a **Mr Rodríguez** (his father's name), not a **Mr Martínez** (his mother's name).
   A **Mrs Hortensia Bussi de Allende** is a **Mrs Allende** (her husband's name), **Bussi** being her maiden name. The **de** is dropped.

A **Miss Lídia Portillo Díaz** is a **Miss Portillo** (her father's name), not a **Miss Díaz** (her mother's name).

Common accented Spanish surnames are: **Núñez, Ordóñez, Yáñez, Zúñiga**.

Some common names and words:

Aerolíneas Argentinas	Argentine national airline
Raúl Alfonsín	former Argentine president
Banco Español de Crédito	
Simón Bolívar	
Gabriel García Márquez	Colombian novelist
Joan Miró	Catalan artist
El Niño	meteorological phenomena
El País	Spanish newspaper
Juan Perón	once president of Argentina
Telefónica	Spanish telecoms company

spectrum means a range of values (as in wavelengths of light) which by infinitesimal changes result in different phenomena, eg, red and violet. **Range** may be more appropriate.

speciality has not yet been replaced by the American **specialty**.

spend is a verb not a noun.

split infinitives

"Would you convey my compliments to the purist who reads your proofs and tell him or her that I write in a sort of broken-down patois which is something like the way a Swiss waiter talks, and that when I split an infinitive, God damn it, I split it so it will stay split."

(Letter from Raymond Chandler to Edward Weeks, 1947.)

In the greyer world of the FT infinitives should be split only if your meaning cannot otherwise be conveyed precisely.

Our object is to further cement trade relations is surely preferable to **Our object is further to cement**.... The second leaves it doubtful about whether an additional object or additional cementing is intended. This example is taken from *Fowler's Modern English Usage*, whose essay on the subject (pp579–582) is strongly recommended; so is Philip Howard's article in *A Word in Time* (pp49–56)

As Fowler says: "We will split infinitives sooner than be ambiguous or artificial."

119

Subeditors should treat them as an umpire treats leg before wicket appeals: most are rejected but an occasional one upheld.

spokesman, **spokeswoman** are best avoided, **spokesperson** abominable. Write **ICI said** rather than **an ICI spokesman said**.

Wherever possible quotations should be attributed to named individuals or as narrowly as possible; thus **the energy efficiency office** rather than **an energy department official**; **energy department** rather than **Whitehall official**. If you can name a spokesman, do so.

sporting scores

cricket: **123 for one**; Smith took **six for 75**.
tennis: **6-2, 9-7, 6-7, 6-0**, the winner's score first.
golf: holes are **3rd, 14th**; match play results **4 and 3**, etc.
football: **2-0**; **Liverpool v Manchester United**.

See also **betting odds**.

stadiums not **stadia** is the plural of **stadium**.

states, **provinces**, **counties and regions** A selective list is on pages 214–220.

stationery is what you write on; **stationary** is not moving

Stationery Office abbreviation is **SO** not **HMSO**.

stealth bomber such as the F-117 is lower case because it refers to a class (like the cruise missile).

stigmas is the plural of **stigma**, unless you are writing about **stigmata** in an ecclesiastical or botanical sense.

stock exchange has initial capitals only when used as part of a title: **London Stock Exchange**.

stock market is two words.

stops in punctuation Use stops to aid clarity rather than in slavish obedience to grammatical rules.

commas Use a comma to join two complete sentences or long clauses.

In a sequence of items do not put a comma before **and** unless leaving it out would lead to ambiguity: **The Bishops of London, Bath and Wells, and Manchester.** (But **the Bishops of London, Winchester and Exeter.**)

There is no need to use a comma in a short phrase at the start of a sentence: **On June 20 the group revealed...**; **But the difficulty of this approach...**

Use two commas in such sentences as: **Mr Brown added, however, that the two events were not connected.**

But avoid sprinkling your copy with so many commas that the flow is interrupted. Keith Waterhouse in *Waterhouse on Newspaper Style* refers to the "asthmatic comma" helping a sentence "get its breath back". There is no way that a sprinkling of commas can rescue a badly constructed sentence.

Commas can be omitted from defining clauses:

> **The schoolboy who pulled an injured driver from his blazing car was praised by police yesterday.**

But beware. A US paper ran the following:

> **Buckingham Palace said that Prince Andrew, son of Queen Elizabeth and a navy helicopter pilot, would sail with the Invincible.**

semicolons The semicolon is useful if you have a series of clauses running in parallel and wish to give greater emphasis than by commas. **The law can be invoked where a crime is suspected; where conflicts, however small, arise; and where the general interest is threatened.** Once you have embarked on such a list using semicolons, you have to stay with it; do not be tempted to use a comma before the final **and**.

Consider this sentence: **Institutional investors include Nomura, the Japanese securities house, General Electric Capital of the US, the French Suez group and Charterhouse, the UK merchant bank, which together with two other institutions took a total 25 per cent stake in Matushka in September 1989.** It is not apparent whether the **which** refers to Charterhouse only or to all the institutions mentioned. Placing semicolons after **house; US; group;** helps but still does not entirely get rid of the ambiguity.

colons The function of the colon, in Fowler's words, is that of "delivering the goods that have been invoiced in the preceding words": **The selector switch has four positions: disc, radio, CD and tape.** The colon can often be substituted for **ie, that is**, etc.

It is also used to introduce direct quotes: **A Lloyd's agent said: "I just do not know where the funds will come from."**

full stops Use a lot. They make sentences easy to read and understand. Gowers says:

"If you can write long sentences that you are satisfied really merit that description, by all means surprise and delight your readers with one occasionally. But the short ones are safer."

A 1993 splash started:

The draft white paper on the future of Britain's coal industry has passed over most of the main recommendations of the Commons trade and industry committee in favour of an alternative plan to expand the market without new legislation.
A case for a rewrite or at least some constructive subbing.

See also **tapeworm sentences.**

question marks These should be used for direct questions only. They must not be used in headlines.
See also **apostrophes, blobs, brackets, quotation marks.**

story is what journalists call an article in the paper. In cross references write **earlier report** not **earlier story**, for example.

Strait of Dover is correct, not **Straits**; similarly **Strait of Gibraltar**.

Strasbourg is a city in France on the Rhine; it is the seat of the European Parliament.

Stratford-upon-Avon is also sometimes spelt **Stratford-on-Avon**.

street fighter is to be avoided as a description of businessmen, politicians, etc, however true it may be.

sub- as a prefix is usually joined to the word that follows: **subcommittee, subcontinent, subcontract, subeditor, subhuman, submachinegun.**

substitute means to **put in place of another** not to take the place of another.

subjunctives In a hypothetical clause prefer **were** to **was**: **If she were to buy the shares**...

summit, when it refers to a meeting, should only be used to describe that between heads of government. Avoid **mini-summit**.

summon, summons A person is **summoned** by receiving a **summons**.

superlatives should be used with great care. Are you certain that the takeover bid is the largest for 20 years? Is Mr Green really the world's third richest person? Was Acme Microchips the first company to produce a 128-bit memory chip? If there is the slightest doubt fall back on a safer form of words (**one of the largest**....).

supersede not **supercede**.

Surinam is a country in South America, formerly Dutch Guiana.

swap not **swop**.

symposia is the plural of **symposium**.

Szczecin is a port in Poland; its German name is **Stettin**.

T

T-shirt is preferred to **tee-shirt**.

table In the US a bill that is **tabled** is shelved or killed. This is opposite to British use; therefore try to use another word or phrase such as **propose**, **introduce**, **put forward**.

Taipei is the capital of Taiwan.

Taiwanese names *see* **Chinese names**.

Tajikistan is a former Soviet republic in central Asia.

takeover is a noun, **to take over** is the verb.

talk People talk **to** not **with** each other.

tandem The phrase **in tandem** means one behind another; if you mean together, write **in parallel**.

taoiseach is the Irish prime minister.

tapeworm sentence In German this is a *Bandwurmsatz*, some examples of which were recorded by the late Wolf Luetkens, a former FT foreign news editor and leader writer. A few examples are listed below; the names have been changed.

However, Gen Verdi, defence minister and the Ruritanian strong man since the annulment of the second round this week of the elections that might well have put the fundamentalist Salvation Front in power, was also a member of the short-lived High Security Council and presumably was important in the dramatic decision to recall Mr Blanco.

Short-term, the crisis can only deepen if the security situation deteriorates when guerrillas, as is probable, greet any reforms with further violence in a bid to provoke reprisals.

Ruritania launched renewed air and artillery attacks on southern Transylvania yesterday after a Ruritanian town was hit by rockets fired across the border by militiamen seeking revenge for the killing of Bishop Weissbraun, leader of the country's Christian fundamentalist organisation.

target has a number of specific meanings but is also used where **objective, purpose, goal** or **ambition** would be better; it is not possible to **fight for, achieve** or **obtain** a target. A construction project is more likely to be **on schedule** than **on target. Target** is a noun but preferably not a verb. If you have to use it as a verb the past tense is spelt **targeted.**

Tattersalls is the UK bloodstock agency.

tautology A Labour party official said the plan was an election-winning budget that would kill dead the claim that Labour was the party of high taxation.

As opposed to only partly killing it, of course.

Tautology is the use of words that merely repeat what has already been said. **Weather conditions** is tautologous; so are **close down, cut back, end up, equally as, finish up, in between, join together, joint co-operation, link together, mutual agreement, mutual co-operation, new departure, now remains, open up, outside of, pair of twins, past history, temporary respite, time-scale.**

Be careful also not to write successive sentences or paragraphs that merely repeat what has already been said.

taxes have no hyphens or capital letters: **council tax, income tax, valued added tax (VAT), capital transfer tax (CTT).**

Tbilisi is the capital of Georgia; prefer this spelling to **Tiflis** or **T'bilisi.**

teargas in one word, not hyphenated.

Teesside, north-east England, has no hyphen.

Tehran, capital of Iran, not **Teheran.**

television TV is acceptable in headings and company names. Principal names **BBC1, BBC2, ITN, ITV, Channel 4, BSkyB, S4C.** Note the spelling of television abbreviations **Pal, Mac, C-Mac, D-Mac.**

teletext is a way of providing information to subscribers on TV sets equipped with a decoder; the BBC's is **Ceefax**, ITV's is **Teletext UK**.

temperatures Write **24°C, 75°F**; prefer centigrade (celsius) to fahrenheit in text. A conversion table is on page 196.

tempi is the plural of **tempo**.

terrorists *see* **bias**.

Thai names tend to be long and the reporter needs to know which is the surname: **Mr Kitti Dumnernchanwanit** followed by **Mr Kitti**.

that As a relative pronoun **that** is often omitted: **The book (that) I am reading**.

Be careful about this: **Mr Brown warned the remaining elements of the former regime would now concentrate on attempting to assassinate the government leaders**. At first reading Mr Brown appears to be issuing a warning to the remaining elements of the former regime; the reader has to read the sentence again to realise that he was warning about what these people might do. **Mr Brown warned that the remaining elements of the former regime would now concentrate on attempting to assassinate the government leaders** leaves no room for doubt.

Another example: **Mr Brown said that he did not believe Mr Green was ignorant of the situation**. Removing **that** would give the first nine words a wholly unintended sense.

That is normally used in a defining clause: **This is the story that Brown wrote**; while **which** is used in informative clauses: **This story, which Brown wrote, is rubbish**.

Avoid such phrases as **not that clever, not that much**; prefer **not so very clever, not so very much** or **not to that extent**.

See also **which**.

the then This is a very ugly construction, which can always be avoided.

Words such as: **the then home secretary, Mr William Whitelaw** can be simply recast by removing the word **then** since it will be obvious from the context that the holder of the office at the time is meant rather than the present home secretary. Extra clarification may be needed when the person referred to has been ennobled: ...**the home secretary, Mr William Whitelaw, now Lord Whitelaw**.

But if there is any doubt about this, write: **Mr William Whitelaw, home secretary at the time** or **the home secretary of the day**.

Thessaloniki is a city and port in Greece; English names **Salonika** or **Salonica**.

third world should if possible be replaced by a term such as **developing countries**. It referred to the poorer countries of Asia, Africa and Latin America. The second world consisted of the former communist countries of Europe.

threshold has only one **h** in the middle.

Tiananmen Square in Beijing, China; the scene of the massacre of protesting students by the People's Liberation Army in June 1989.

Tigray, province of Ethiopia, not **Tigre**.

Timbuktu is a town in Mali; the French spelling is **Timbouctou**.

time   The 12 hour clock should be used: **1am, 9.30pm**. Normally local time is used, but in foreign stories the **Greenwich Mean Time (GMT)** equivalent may be given if it adds to the story.

British Summer Time (BST) is GMT plus 1 hour; Central European Time (CET) is GMT plus 1 hour; Eastern Standard Time (EST) is GMT minus 5 hours.

Be careful when referring to time past: **Wednesday's trade figures** should not be used to refer to figures published on Wednesday; the figures themselves are probably last month's or last year's. Similarly, prefer **the meeting at the weekend** to **the weekend's meeting** so that we can still employ weekend as an adjective where it has some meaning (eg, **weekend jaunt, weekend cottage, weekend affair**).

timeshare is one word, not hyphenated.

titles   *see* **names and titles**

told the Financial Times should only be used where a reporter believes he or she has been given information that is unavailable to other media. Do not use the phrase to describe information obtained at a press conference.

top in the sense of important, senior, highly placed, is often used meaninglessly to impress the reader. Avoid it.

tornadoes is the plural of **tornado**.

torpedoes is the plural of **torpedo**.

Tote is the common name for the **Horserace Totalisator Board**.

trade names must start with a capital letter; if they do not the manufacturers write to us.

Do not use proprietary names as general words. A few are listed below with a suitable generic alternative.

Astroturf	artificial grass
Biro	ballpoint pen
Calor gas	bottled gas
Fibreglass	glass fibre
Formica	laminate
Hoover	vacuum cleaner
Jacuzzi	whirlpool bath
Photostat	photocopier
Portakabin	portable building
Thermos*	vacuum flask
Kitemark†	certification mark

*Thermos is a legal generic in the US but not in the UK.
†The Kitemark is a registered trademark of the BSI, the standards organisation. It should not be used in referring to the seal of approval of any non-BSI scheme.

Remember the initial capital on: **Coke, Dictaphone, Jeep, Monotype, Perspex, Plasticine, Polaroid, Pyrex, Sellotape, Technicolor, Teflon, Terylene, Vaseline, Velcro, Xerox, Yellow Pages**.

trade unions A selective list is on pages 225–226.

tradeable not **tradable**.

Trades Union Congress is the association of British trade unions (not **Trade Union**...).

trafficker is someone who traffics in something.

Trans Dnestr is a region of Moldova.

transatlantic, transpacific are lower case, no hyphens; **trans** followed by other place names, such as **trans-Siberian**, should be hyphenated.

Transcaucasia is the larger part of Caucasia in the extreme south-east of Europe. The smaller part is known as the **Caucasus** (formerly Ciscaucasia). Transcaucasia consists of **Georgia, Armenia** and **Azerbaijan**.

trillion is a million million or a thousand billion; it is normally used only in referring to oil and gas output, sometimes to lire. Prefer **1,400bn** to **1.4 trillion**.

tsar not **czar**.

Turkish names Although Turkish is written in a modified Latin script, westerners and others have preferred to use phonetic or traditional spellings for simplicity. Turkish uses a number of accents such as the dotless **ı**, **ö** and **ü**. Accents are also used on some capital letters, but this practice should not be followed in the FT for technical reasons.

Some common names and words:

Atatürk	Süleyman Demirel	Koç *industrial group*
Rauf Denktas	Dŏgan Güres	Turgut Ozal

Turkmenistan is a former Soviet republic in central Asia, bordering the Caspian Sea.

turnround as a noun is one word.

Tuvalu is a group of islands in the south-west Pacific; former name the **Ellice Islands**.

Tyrol in Austria, not **Tirol**. Note that part of **East Tyrol** is in Italy.

U

Ukraine is the name of the country, *not* **the Ukraine**. A Ukrainian living in Canada writes to the FT every time we get this wrong.

Ukrainian names The spelling of Ukrainian proper and place names can be confusing. Before the collapse of the Soviet Union Ukrainian words were traditionally translated into Russian and then transliterated into English. Now Ukrainians prefer to transliterate directly from Ukrainian.

Many common Ukrainian names differ from the Russian versions: **Mykhailo** rather than **Mikhail**, **Mykola** rather than **Nikolai**, **Volodymyr** rather than **Vladimir**. One difference to watch for is the letter **g** which is common in Russian but rare in Ukrainian. Thus a Ukrainian is **Olha** not **Olga**.

With the exception of a few places which have established English spellings, the Ukrainian transliteration should be used: **Lviv** not **Lvov**, **Rivne** not **Rovno**, **Ivano-Frankivsk** not **Ivano-Frankovsk**.

The main exceptions are: **Kiev** not **Kiv**, **Odessa** not **Odesa**, the river **Dnepr** not **Dnipro**, **Chernobyl** not **Chornobil**.

Ulster *see* **Ireland**.

Umlaut is the German accent made up of two dots. It is sometimes used on the letter **a** (**Tannhäuser**); **o** (**Pöhl**); **u** (**Führer**). On capital letters it is replaced by an **e** following the inflected letter: *TANNHAEUSER*, **POEHL, FUEHRER**.

Umm al Quwain is a member state of the United Arab Emirates.

under way is correct not underway.

undersecretary is one word.

unexceptionable means beyond criticism or objection; **unexceptional** means ordinary or normal.

United Kingdom is England, Wales, Scotland and Northern Ireland. Great Britain is England, Scotland and Wales.

United Nations High Commissioner for Refugees is an organisation and thus has initial capitals. It can be referred to as a UN agency and abbreviates to **UNHCR**.

up-market is hyphenated but is best avoided.

utilise Use is shorter.

Uzbekistan is a former Soviet republic in central Asia.

V

Vanuata is a group of islands in the south-west Pacific, formerly known as the **New Hebrides**.

VAT *see* **taxes**.

verbal Any agreement is verbal: it consists of words; one that is not written down is **oral**.

vetoes is the plural of **veto**.

viable means capable of separate existence; it comes from the French *vie* not the Latin *via*. **Durable, workable, lasting, effective, practicable, profitable** are all possible alternatives.

vice- is hyphenated in titles: **vice-president, vice-chancellor**.

vice versa is two words.

video is acceptable shorthand for videotape or a video recording.

videocassette, videodisc are not hyphenated.

videotex provides two-way communication via telephone lines enabling provision of services such as home banking and shopping.

Vietnamese names People have two or three names, the last one being the surname: **Mr Nguyen Mai** followed by **Mr Mai**. Many people are called **Nguyen**, which can be either first name or surname.

virtuosi is the plural of **virtuoso**.

volcanos is the plural of **volcano**.

W

Wall Street is an acceptable term for the financial community of New York. The **The** of The Wall Street Journal is capitalised.

war is lower case: **first/second world war** (not **World War I/II**); **Falklands war, Gulf war, cold war**.

warn is a transitive verb; use **give warning** or **warn somebody**; some licence is permitted in headings.

warplane is not as specific as **bomber, fighter**, etc.

well known Beware: if someone is well known there is no need to say so; if he or she is not it is a lie.

West Bank of the Jordan; use initial capitals.

which informs while **that** defines is the best rule to follow. **This is the car that was involved in an accident** but **This car, which was in an accident, is a write-off**. Note that the **which** clause needs commas.

The second example can stand by itself even if the non-defining **which** clause is removed; in the first example **that** cannot be removed without recasting the sentence.

whisky is Scotch; **whiskey** is Irish, rye or bourbon.

white paper and **green paper** are lower case.

whose The possessive form of the relative pronoun can refer to both people and things: **GEC, whose results failed to meet expectations**; to write **GEC, the results of which**... would be extraordinarily clumsy. Whose (inanimate) is quite acceptable.

Windermere in Cumbria; do not write **Lake Windermere**.

wines *see* **drink**.

withhold has two **h's** in the middle.

Wolfe's Law of Journalism.

> You cannot hope
> to bribe or twist,
> thank God! the
> British Journalist.
> But, seeing what
> the man will do
> unbribed, there's
> no occasion to.
> (*Humbert Wolfe, 1930*)

A grave libel of course.

women should be called what they wish to be called (**Miss, Ms, Mrs**), writing **Ms** when in doubt. *See also* **bias**.

Worldwide Fund for Nature was once called the World Wildlife Fund.

wrack and ruin is preferred to **rack and ruin**; even better would be not to use the phrase at all.

writedown as a noun is one word.

XYZ

years Be specific about what sort of year you are referring to: **calendar year, crop year, financial year, tax year.**

Yekaterinburg in Russia, not **Yekaterinaburg** or **Ekaterinburg.**

Yemen not **the Yemen.**

YT is **Youth Training**, formerly the YTS.

Yugoslavia has changed and is still changing; consult the FT's Foreign desk if in doubt. The components of former Yugoslavia are listed on page 219–220.

zero the plural is zeros.

zeugma He took his hat and his departure.

REFERENCE
SECTION

ABBREVIATIONS

Common abbreviations are listed here. The full form should normally be used at first mention, the abbreviation subsequently. Where it is not necessary to use the full form at all the name appears within square brackets: **[British Broadcasting Corporation]**. Sometimes an explanatory phrase will obviate the need to spell out the whole title: **the conciliation service Acas**.

Words in round brackets are for information only and do not form part of an organisation's title.

ABM	anti-ballistic-missile missile
Acas	Advisory, Conciliation and Arbitration Service
ACT	advance corporation tax
	Australian Capital Territory
ADR	American Depositary Receipt
AGM	annual general meeting
AGR	advanced gas-cooled reactor
AIBD	Association of International Bond Dealers
Aids	acquired immune deficiency syndrome
Amex	American Stock Exchange (New York)
ANC	African National Congress
AP	Associated Press
Apec	Asia Pacific Economic Co-operation group
APR	annual percentage rate
ASA	Advertising Standards Authority
ASB	Accounting Standards Board
Ascii	American Standard Code for Information Interchange
Asean	Association of South East Asian Nations
Asic	application specific integrated circuit
AT&T	American Telephone and Telegraph
Awacs	airborne warning and control system
b/d	barrels a day
BA	British Airways
BAe	British Aerospace
Bafta	British Academy of Film and Television Arts
BBC	[British Broadcasting Corporation]

BCCI	Bank of Credit and Commerce International
BIS	Bank for International Settlements
BMA	British Medical Association
Bq	becquerel
BSE	bovine spongiform encephalopathy
BSI	British Standards Institution
BST	British Summer Time
BTec	Business and Technician Education Council
Btu	British thermal unit
Bupa	British United Provident Association
C&W	Cable and Wireless
CA	Consumers' Association
CAA	Civil Aviation Authority (UK)
CAB	Citizens' Advice Bureau
Cad	computer-aided design
CAP	Common Agricultural Policy
Caricom	Caribbean Community and Common Market

CB	citizens' band radio
CBI	Confederation of British Industry
cc	cubic centimetre
CCA	current cost accounting
c/d	certificate of deposit
CD	compact disc
CDU	Christian Democratic Union (Germany)
CET	Central European Time
CFCs	chlorofluorocarbons
CFE	Conventional Forces in Europe
CGE	Compagnie Générale d'Electricité
CGT	capital gains tax
CIA	Central Intelligence Agency (US)
CID	Criminal Investigation Department
cif	cost, insurance and freight included
CIS	Commonwealth of Independent States
CND	Campaign for Nuclear Disarmament
COB	Commission des Opérations de Bourse
Cocom	Co-ordinating Committee on Multilateral Export Controls
COI	Central Office of Information
Consob	Commissione Nazionale per la Societa e la Borsa
CPP	current purchasing power accounting
CPU	central processing unit (computer)
CSA	Child Support Agency
CSCE	Conference on Security and Co-operation in Europe
CSO	Central Statistics Office
CSU	Christian Social Union (Germany)
CTT	capital transfer tax
DEA	Drug Enforcement Administration (US)
DNA	[deoxyribonucleic acid]
DoE	Department of the Environment
Dos	disc operating system
DSS	Department of Social Security
DTB	Deutsche Terminbörse
DTI	Department of Trade and Industry
DTP	desktop publishing
dwt	deadweight tonnes
EBRD	European Bank for Reconstruction and Development *not BERD*

ECGD	Export Credits Guarantee Department (UK)
Ecowas	Economic Community of West African States
Ecu	European currency unit
EFA	European Fighter Aircraft
EFT	electronic funds transfer
Efta	European Free Trade Association
eftpos	electronic funds transfer at point of sale
eg	for example
EIB	European Investment Bank
EISA	extended industry standard architecture
EMS	European Monetary System
Emu	economic and monetary union
EPA	Environmental Protection Agency (US)
ERM	exchange rate mechanism (of the European Monetary System)
ESA	European Space Agency
Esop	employee share ownership plan
EST	Eastern Standard Time
EU	European Union
Euratom	European Atomic Energy Commission
Eutelsat	European Telecommunications Satellite Organisation
FAA	Federal Aviation Administration (US)
FAO	Food and Agriculture Organisation
FBI	Federal Bureau of Investigation
FCO	Foreign and Commonwealth Office
FDA	Food and Drug Administration (US)
FDP	Free Democratic party (Germany)
Fed	Federal Reserve Board (US)
Fifa	[International Association Football Federation]
Fifo	first in first out
Fimbra	Financial Intermediaries, Managers and Brokers Regulatory Association (UK)
FNMA	Federal National Mortgage Association (Fannie Mae) (US)
fob	free on board
G7	Group of Seven
Gatt	General Agreement on Tariffs and Trade
GCHQ	Government Communication Headquarters
GCSE	General Certificate of Secondary Education

142

GCC	Gulf Co-operation Council
GDP	gross domestic product
GE	General Electric Company (of the US)
GEC	General Electric Company (of the UK)
GNP	gross national product
grt	gross registered tonnes
Gui	graphical user interface
HDTV	high-definition television
HGV	heavy goods vehicle
HIV	human immunodeficiency virus
Holmes	[Home Office Large Major Enquiry System]
HSE	Health and Safety Executive (UK)
IADB	Inter-American Development Bank
IAEA	International Atomic Energy Agency
Iata	International Air Transport Association
IBM	International Business Machines
IC	integrated circuit
ICBM	intercontinental ballistic missile
ICI	Imperial Chemical Industries
ICRC	International Committee of the Red Cross
IDA	International Development Association
IEA	International Energy Agency
IFC	International Finance Corporation
Ifo	(German) economics institute (Munich)
ILO	International Labour Organisation
IMF	International Monetary Fund
Imro	Investment Management Regulatory Organisation
Inmarsat	International Maritime Satellite Organisation
Insee	Institute of Economic Statistics (Paris)
Intelsat	International Telecommunications Satellite Consortium
IOC	International Olympic Committee
IoJ	Institute of Journalists
IOR	Istituto per le Opere di Religione
IRA	[Irish Republican Army]
IRS	Internal Revenue Service (US)
ISA	industry standard architecture
ISBN	International Standard Book Number
ISDN	integrated services digital network
ISO	International Standards Organisation

IT	information technology
ITA	Independent Television Authority
IWC	International Whaling Commission
Jessi	Joint European Submicron Silicon Initiative
Jr	junior
kB	kilobyte
kg	kilogramme
kHz	kilohertz
km	kilometre
km/h	kilometres per hour
Lan	local area network
Lautro	Life Assurance and Unit Trust Regulatory Association (UK)
LBO	leveraged buyout
LCD	liquid crystal display
LDC	less developed country
LEA	local education authority
LED	light-emitting diode
Libid	London Interbank Bid Rate
Libor	London Interbank Offered Rate
Liffe	London International Financial Futures Exchange
Lifo	last in first out
LME	London Metal Exchange
LNG	liquefied natural gas
London Fox	London Futures and Options Exchange
LPG	liquefied petroleum gas
LPO	London Philharmonic Orchestra
LSD	[lysergic acid diethylamide]
LSE	London School of Economics
LSO	London Symphony Orchestra
M&S	Marks and Spencer
Matif	Marche à Terme Internationale de France
MB	megabyte
MCA	monetary compensation amount
	microchannel architecture
ME	myalgic encephalomyelitis
MEP	member of the European Parliament

144

MFA	Multi-Fibre Arrangement
MFN	most favoured nation
MGN	Mirror Group Newspapers
Miras	mortgage interest relief at source
Mirv	multiple independently targetable re-entry vehicle
MIT	Massachusetts Institute of Technology
Miti	Ministry of International Trade and Industry (Japan)
MLR	minimum lending rate
MMC	Monopolies and Mergers Commission (UK)
MoD	Ministry of Defence
MoT	Ministry of Transport
MP	member of parliament
MPEG	Moving Picture Experts Group
mpg, mph	miles per gallon, miles per hour
MRCA	multi-role combat aircraft
MS	multiple sclerosis
Nafta	North American Free Trade Agreement
Nasa	National Aeronautics and Space Administration (US)
Nasdaq	National Association of Securities Dealers Automated Quotation System
Nato	[North Atlantic Treaty Organisation]
NCB	National Coal Board
NHS	National Health Service
NUJ	National Union of Journalists
NUM	National Union of Mineworkers
O&Y	Olympia and York
Oapec	Organisation of Arab Petroleum Exporting Countries
OAS	Organisation of American States
OAU	Organisation of African Unity
OCR	optical character recognition
OECD	Organisation for Economic Co-operation and Development
Offer	Office of Electricity Regulation
Ofgas	Office of Gas Supply
OFT	Office of Fair Trading
Oftel	Office of Telecommunications
Ofwat	Office of Water Services
OIC	Organisation of the Islamic Conference
Opec	Organisation of Petroleum Exporting Countries

Opraf	Office of Passenger Rail Franchising
OTC	over the counter
Oxfam	[Oxford Committee for Famine Relief]
P&O	[Peninsular and Oriental Steam Navigation]
p/e	price/earnings ratio
Pal	[phase alternate time] (TV standard)
PC	personal computer
	political correctness
Pcas	Polytechnics Central Admissions System
Pep	personal equity plan
Pin	personal identification number
plc	public limited company
PLO	Palestine Liberation Organisation
PPS	parliamentary private secretary
PR	proportional representation
	public relations
PRT	petroleum revenue tax
PSBR	public sector borrowing requirement
PTT	post, telegraph and telephone
PWR	pressurised water reactor
Quango	[quasi-autonomous non-governmental organisation]
R&D	research and development
Ram	random access memory
RAM	Royal Academy of Music
RCM	Royal College of Music
RHA	regional health authority
Rico	Racketeers Influenced and Corrupt Organisation (US)
Risc	reduced instruction set computing
RNLI	Royal National Lifeboat Institution
ro-ro	roll on-roll off
Rom	read only memory
Rosco	rolling stock leasing company
RPI	retail price index
rpm	revolutions per minute
RSC	Royal Shakespeare Company
RSI	repetitive strain (or stress) injury
RUC	Royal Ulster Constabulary
S&L	savings and loan company (US)
S-Ram	static Ram

Salt	Strategic Arms Limitation Talks
Sam	surface-to-air missile
SAS	Special Air Service Regiment
SDLP	Social Democratic and Labour party
SDR	Special Drawing Right
Seaq	Stock Exchange Automated Quotation System
SEC	Securities and Exchange Commission (US)
Serps	state earnings-related pension scheme (UK)
SFO	Serious Fraud Office (UK)
Shape	Supreme Headquarters Allied Powers Europe
SIB	Securities and Investments Board (UK)
SPD	Social Democratic party (Germany)
SRO	self-regulatory organisation (UK)
SSSI	site of special scientific interest
SST	supersonic transport
Stol	short take-off and landing
Tesco	train engineering service company
Tessa	tax exempt special savings account
TNT	[trinitrotoluene]
TOC	train-operating company
TOU	train-operating unit
TUC	Trades Union Congress
UAE	United Arab Emirates
UBS	Union Bank of Switzerland
UCCA	Universities' Central Council on Admissions
UDA	Ulster Defence Association
UDR	Ulster Defence Regiment
Uefa	[Union of European Football Associations]
Ufo	unidentified flying object
UHF	ultra high frequency
UKAEA	United Kingdom Atomic Energy Authority
ULCC	ultra large crude carrier
UK	United Kingdom
Unctad	United Nations Conference on Trade and Development
Unesco	United Nations Educational, Scientific and Cultural Organisation
UNHCR	United Nations High Commissioner for Refugees
Unicef	United Nations Children's Fund

UPC	Universal Product Code
US	[United States]
USM	unlisted securities market (UK)
VAT	valued added tax
VDT/VDU	visual display terminal/unit
VHF	very high frequency
VLCC	very large crude carrier
VLSI	very large-scale integration
Vtol	vertical take-off and landing
Wan	wide area network
WEU	Western European Union
WHO	World Health Organisation
Wipo	World Intellectual Property Organisation
xd	ex-dividend
YT	Youth Training (UK)

See also **Organisations**, pages 200–211; **Trade unions**, pages 225–226.

COMMODITIES TERMS GLOSSARY

Note: Most terms should be defined on first mention.

arabica/robusta types of coffee bean.

backwardation is used when prices for cash delivery are higher than for forward delivery. The opposite of **contango** (*see below*).

borrowing a term used mainly on the London Metal Exchange to describe the purchase of cash spot or supplies to be delivered close to the present date against the simultaneous sale of a matching quantity at a future date. This is also known as **cash-and-carry**. *See also* **lending.**

bullion this is usually precious metal in non-coined form: ingots, bars etc; it may also be used for other metals, particularly lead.

carat a measure of the fineness of gold. Pure gold is 24 carat; thus 19 carat gold is 19 parts gold and five of alloy. The term is also used as a weight for precious stones: 1 carat equals 200 milligrams.

contango is used when prices for future delivery are higher than those for cash or spot transactions. The gap between a cash price and a forward quotation is often based on current interest rates plus storage and insurance costs to cover the cost of holding the commodity for the relevant period. The opposite is **backwardation** (*see above*).

fixing the daily meetings of London bullion brokers to agree prices of gold (twice a day) and silver (once).

hedging the method of obtaining protection against unpredictable price fluctuations by taking equal and opposite positions in physicals (a quantity of a commodity available for immediate delivery) and futures (a quantity available for delivery at a specified future date). It is also used to describe a general protection against unpredictable developments (exchange rate movements, failure of supplies).

lending a London Metal Exchange term for sale of cash metal (or a future close to the present date) with a simultaneous purchase of a matching amount for delivery at a future date. *See also* **borrowing.**

limit the maximum price fluctuation allowed in certain commodities or securities markets within one trading session. If the limit is breached the regulations require that trading must cease for a period. **Limit up** means the limit is breached by a rise in prices; **limit down** by a fall.

liquidation the cancellation of an open position (either a previous purchase or a sale) on a futures market. It normally describes sales of outstanding purchases.

long an outstanding purchase of a commodity for future or present delivery. Traders go long if they believe prices will rise.

lot the minimum dealing unit in a futures market.

margin call the demand by a broker to a client to increase his margin or the deposit which is required to make a transaction. This is usually because a potential loss seems more likely or larger than previously expected. Markets or clearing houses set compulsory margin requirements, which may be varied.

Multi-Fibre Arrangement the arrangment signed by 50 countries in 1973 under the auspices of Gatt which lays down rules for trade in textile products.

nearby delivery the month on a futures contract nearest to the date for which delivery of the commodity is specified.

open interest the number of contracts, bought or sold, not offset by a matching transaction of an opposite type.

pit the area where futures are traded on a commodity exchange. It is particularly used to describe the place where grain futures are traded in Chicago.

ring the area used for trading at, for example, the London Metal Exchange, where only elected ring-dealing members are allowed to trade.

settlement price the average price at the close of the day's trading. It is used to set the next day's fluctuation limits and to determine margin calls on futures contracts. At the London Metal Exchange the settlement is the morning official offer price.

short the sale of a commodity future in expectation of a fall in prices.

soft commodity non-metal commodities.

spot market the trading of physical commodities for immediate or very near delivery as opposed to contracts on a futures exchange.

spot price the cash price of a commodity immediately available for delivery.

spread the gap in a quotation between buying and selling prices of a commodity in different months.

squeeze a shortage of supplies available for delivery to the market, which forces up spot prices.

stop loss a mechanism for restricting losses by instructing a broker to buy or sell when a specific price is reached.

twitch the advancing or postponing of a purchase or sale to a different month

warrant or warehouse receipt a receipt given by a warehouse for its holdings of a physical commodity. The warrant is proof of ownership of the commodity and is bought and sold on the futures market.

COMPUTING TERMS GLOSSARY

"To err is human but to really foul things up requires a computer."

(Anon)

Note: Most terms should be defined on first mention.

artificial intelligence programs which mimic human intelligence, most commonly by the use of **expert systems**. The computer is programmed to ask a series of questions similar to those which would be asked by, for example, a doctor or a geologist. Such programs may learn from mistakes and can make complex choices.

Ascii (American Standard Code for Information Interchange) a standard system of representing letters and numbers in digital format. It allows text to be understood by computers of all different types.

baud is a measure of the number of data bits that can be transmitted each second between computers.

bit is a contraction of BInary digiT. It is the smallest unit of information a computer can handle, represented by 0 or 1, ie, on or off.

bug a fault in a program or unexpected effect; to **debug** a program is to cure the faults.

bus a data highway within a computer.

byte a group of eight **bits**. An eight-bit byte can be used to represent a single alphanumeric character. For example, seven bytes are needed to store the word compute.

card a printed circuit board added to a computer to give extra abilities and functions, for example high quality screen graphics.

CD-Rom read only computer memory stored on a compact disc; a CD-Rom disc can store up to 600 megabytes of information. As an example the complete *Oxford English Dictionary* can be stored on a single disc. Computers with CD-Rom drives are **multimedia** *qv* computers.

chips *see* **microchips**

computer-aided design (Cad) allows the drawing, design and testing of ideas on screen.

database an organised collection of data from which information can be extracted by specifying various criteria for selection.

desktop publishing (DTP) design and graphic work carried out on a microcomputer. It combines word processing, graphics and usually a laser printer.

disc operating system (Dos) a program which marshals the internal operations of the computer itself, allocating space in memory for work files, organising movement of data through the system and so on. Mainframes use proprietary operating systems such as IBM's **MVS**; the FT's Edwin runs on Tandem's **Guardian** operating system.

The most popular personal computer operating system is Microsoft's **MS-Dos**, followed by Digital Research's **DR-Dos**. Battle is raging over whether the standard operating system for 32-bit computers should be IBM and Microsoft's **OS/2** or AT&T's **Unix**.

E-mail is an abbreviation of **electronic mail**, mail sent and received by a computer fitted with a modem; messages and data are stored and sent to their destination by a central computer. The term is also used for messages sent on local area networks (**Lan** *qv*) within organisations.

extended industry standard architecture (EISA) standard PC design upgraded to make the best of 32-bit **microchips**, *qv*.

giga thousand million as in gigabyte.

hardware the magnetic, mechanical and electrical components of a computer and peripherals.

hertz or cycles a second a measure of the speed of the internal clock which co-ordinates all the activities within a microprocessor. For example 80/386 **microchips**, *qv*, have clocks running at 25m ticks a second (25MHz).

icon pictorial identifiers used in many programs to replace keyboard commands. *See* **wimp**.

industry standard architecture (ISA) conforming to the design of the IBM PC/AT personal computer.

integrated services digital network (ISDN) telecommunications technology which will eventually replace the modem as a means of communication between computers.

Internet the Internet is a computer network linking businesses, universities, government institutions and private computer users around the world.

local area network (Lan) a low cost, fast and efficient method for connecting personal computers together to share data over a limited area.

mainframe the central processing unit of a large computer, usually receiving input from a number of terminals.

megabyte memory sizes in computers are measured in bytes, so a one megabyte (1MB) computer has a main memory capacity of 8m bits.

memory *see* **RAM** and **ROM**.

micro one millionth, as in microsecond.

microchannel architecture (MCA) IBM's proprietary design for advanced 32-bit computers; in contention with **EISA**, *qv*, as the future standard.

microcomputer a small computer, smaller than a minicomputer and much smaller than a mainframe; the sort that most of us own.

microchips (microprocessor chips) perform the functions of a central processing unit in a small computer. The most important are the new 32-bit chips of which the most popular are Intel's 80/486 and Motorola's 68000 family.

mips millions of instructions per second. A common but misleading measure of computer power.

modem (modulator/demodulator) a device for connecting two computers by a telephone line, requiring a modulator to convert computer signals into audio signals and a demodulator to reverse the process. When telephone networks are completely digital in character (**ISDN** *qv*) modems will be redundant.

motherboard the main printed circuit board in a (usually micro-) computer carrying the central processing unit.

MS-Dos *see* **disc operating system**.

multimedia is a combination of sound, graphics, animation and video; in the world of computers, multimedia usually refers to computers that contain a sound card and a CD-Rom storage device.

multiplexer a device combining the output from a number of sources for transmission down a single communications channel such as a telephone line, thus saving on time and transmission costs.

network a system comprising several terminals with one or more central processing units, allowing several users to draw on the same data. The FT system is a big network.

nano thousand millionth as in nanosecond.

optical character recognition (OCR) a system for reading print into a computer's memory. Sometimes it works.

open systems interconnection (OSI) a set of standards or rules which will enable any computer obeying the rules to be easily connected to any other computer also obeying the rules.

OS/2 *see* **disc operating system**.

peripheral any piece of equipment that does not form part of the **central processing unit**: keyboard, screen, printer, disc drive.

personal computers are measured by the number of **bits**, *qv*, they can handle at a time. Pocket calculators handle four bits at a time, the Apple II handles eight bits at a time, the original IBM PC handled 16 bits at a time and the latest machines based on Intel's 80/486 chip handle 32 bits at a time, just like a mainframe computer.

155

program a set of definitions and instructions to make a computer perform a particular task. Note the spelling. It is a technical term and there are no alternatives.

random access memory (Ram) a memory system in which the stored information can be rewritten many times. The maximum Ram in a 16-bit PC is normally 640K. **D-Ram** is dynamic Ram, memory which requires continuous electric current. **S-Ram** is static Ram, in which the memory contents are retained if the power is switched off.

real-time where the computer and user carry on a dialogue, the computer responding immediately to the user's commands and inquiries; for example, word processing.

read only memory (Rom) a storage device whose contents can be retrieved but not altered by the user or software; it can now be on a compact disc, **CD-Rom** *qv.*

reduced instruction set computing (Risc) a current fashion in the industry for designing comparatively simple chips that operate at blindingly fast speeds – 10 to 20 mips and more.

software the programs that are used with a computer system.

spreadsheet an application program that creates large grids for the entry of numerical and other information and allows their manipulation by mathematical means.

systems network architecture (SNA) a set of standards enabling the connection of IBM systems into networks. Likely to be replaced over time by **open systems interconnection** *qv.*

universal product code (UPC) a bar coding system used in retailing.

Unix *see* **disc operating system.**

virus an illegal implant of coding into a computer's files with the aim of disrupting its activity. **Worms, trojans** and **computer bombs** are other names for types of malicious software

wide area network (Wan) a method of linking computers to share data over long distances.

Wimp (windows, icons, mice, pull-down menus) a user interface developed by Apple Macintosh and designed for easy use by non-specialists.

Windows a user interface designed by Microsoft which duplicates much of the look and feel of Apple Macintosh's Wimp software.

CURRENCIES

The main world currencies and their abbreviations are listed here. The figures quoted are an approximate conversion of £1 at the rates of July 1994.

Where a story contains amounts expressed in foreign currency a sterling conversion is made of the first figure quoted: **DM45bn (£18.4bn)**. On the ICN pages, World Trade Page and in the International Edition the conversion is to a dollar equivalent.

Currencies are expressed as: **£1**; **£2,000–£3,000**; **£2bn–£3bn**; **$10.20**; **50 cents**. There is no space between a currency symbol and the figure that follows, except with the Dutch florin, where a thin space should separate the two.

Currencies marked with an asterisk (*) are tied to the US dollar.

Currencies marked with a double dagger (‡) are too volatile (or in some cases too new) for rough conversions to be made in a style book. Up-to-date values of principal currencies are printed on the FT Currencies page every day. A full list appears in the FT Guide to World Currencies every Monday.

Country	Currency	Abbreviation
Abu Dhabi	UAE dirham	Dh5.7
Afghanistan	afghani	4,000 afghanis
Albania	lek	162leks
Algeria	dinar	AD60
Andorra	French franc	FFr8.3
	peseta	Pta200
Angola	kwanza	Kz150,000
Antigua	E. Caribbean $	EC$4.0
Argentina	peso	1.5 pesos*
Armenia	dram	‡
Australia	Australian dollar	A$2
Austria	Schilling	Sch17
Azerbaijan	manat	‡
Bahamas	Bahama dollar	$1.5*
Bahrain	dinar	BD0.59
Bangladesh	taka	Tk60
Barbados	Barbados dollar	B$3.0
Belarus	rouble	Rbs‡
Belgium	Belgian franc	BFr50

Belize	Belizean dollar	Bz$3.0
Benin	CFA franc	CFA Fr830
Bermuda	Bermuda dollar	$1.5*
Bhutan	ngultrum	Ng46
Bolivia	boliviano	$b7
Bosnia-Hercegovina	new dinar	ND‡
Botswana	pula	P4
Brazil	real	R$1.4
Brunei	Brunei dollar	Br$2.3
Bulgaria	lev	Lv90
Burkina Faso	CFA franc	CFA Fr830
Burma	kyat	Kt9
Burundi	Burundi franc	BuFr400
Cambodia	riel	5,400 riels
Cameroon	CFA franc	CFA Fr830
Canada	Canadian dollar	C$2.0
Cayman Islands	CI dollar	CI$1.2
Central African Republic	CFA franc	CFA Fr830
Chad	CFA franc	CFA Fr830
Chile	peso	650 pesos
China	yuan	Yn13
Colombia	peso	1,300 pesos
CIS	rouble	Rbs3,000‡
Congo	CFA franc	CFA Fr830
Costa Rica	colon	230 colons
Côte d'Ivoire	CFA franc	CFA Fr830
Croatia	kuna	K9
Cuba	peso	1.1 pesos
Cyprus	Cyprus £	C£0.76
Cyprus (north)	Turkish lira	TL50,000
Czech Republic	koruna	Kcs44
Denmark	krone, kroner	DKr10
Djibouti	Djibouti franc	DFr260
Dominica	E. Caribbean $	EC$4.2
Dominican Republic	peso	20 pesos
Ecuador	sucre	3,000 sucres
Egypt	Egyptian pound	E£5

El Salvador	colon	13 colons
Equatorial Guinea	CFA franc	CFA Fr830
Estonia	kroon	EKr20
Ethiopia	birr	8.5 birr
Faroe Islands	Danish krone	DKr10
Fiji	Fiji dollar	F$2.2
Finland	markka	FM8.1
France	franc	FFr8.3
Gabon	CFA franc	CFA Fr830
Gambia	dalasi	15 dalasis
Georgia	coupon	‡
Germany	D-Mark	DM2.4
Ghana	cedi	1,500 cedis
Gibraltar	Gibraltar £	£1
Greece	drachma	Dr370
Greenland	Danish krone	DKr10
Grenada	E. Caribbean $	EC$4.2
Guadaloupe	franc	Fr8.3
Guatemala	quetzal	Q9
Guinea	Guinea franc	GFr1,500
Guinea-Bissau	peso	19,000 pesos
Guyana	Guyana dollar	G$220
Haiti	gourde	18 gourdes
Honduras	lempira	13 lempiras
Hong Kong	Hong Kong dollar	HK$12
Hungary	forint	Ft150
Iceland	krona	IKr105
India	rupee	Rs50
Indonesia	rupiah	Rp3,400
Iran	rial	IR2,500‡
Iraq	dinar	ID0.5
Irish Republic	punt	I£1
Israel	shekel	Shk4.7
Italy	lira, lire	L2,400
Jamaica	Jamaican dollar	J$49
Japan	yen	Y155
Jordan	dinar	JD1

Kazakhstan	tenge	‡
Kenya	shilling	Ks90
Korea, North	won	Won3.2
Korea, South	won	Won1,200
Kuwait	dinar	KD0.46
Kyrgyzstan	som	‡
Laos	new kip	K1,100
Latvia	lats	0.85 lats
Lebanon	Lebanese pound	L£2,500
Lesotho	maluti	5.7 maluti
Liberia	Liberian dollar	L$1.5*
Libya	dinar	LD0.48
Liechtenstein	Swiss franc	SFr2.1
Lithuania	litas	6.2 litas
Luxembourg	Lux franc	LFr50
Macao	pataca	12 patacas
Macedonia	new dinar	ND‡
Madagascar	Malagasy franc	MgFr5,000
Malawi	kwacha	K11
Malaysia	Malaysian dollar	M$4
Maldive Islands	rufiya	18 rufiyas
Mali	CFA franc	CFA Fr830
Malta	lira	LM0.58
Martinique	franc	MFr8.3
Mauritania	ouguiya	190 ouguiya
Mauritius	rupee	MRs27
Mexico	peso	5 pesos
Moldova	leu,lei	‡
Monaco	French franc	FFr8.3
Mongolia	tugrik	600 tugriks
Montserrat	E. Caribbean $	EC$4.2
Morocco	dirham	Dh14
Mozambique	metical, meticais	9,000 meticais
Namibia	S. African rand	R5.7
Nepal	rupee	NRs77
Netherlands	guilder	Fl 2.8
Neth Antilles	guilder	NAFl 2.8
New Zealand	NZ dollar	NZ$2.6m

161

Nicaragua	gold cordoba	10 cordobas
Niger	CFA franc	CFA Fr830
Nigeria	naira	N34
Norway	krone, kroner	NKr11
Oman	riyal	OR0.6
Pakistan	rupee	Rs45
Panama	balboa	$1.5*
Papua New Guinea	kina	K1.5
Paraguay	guarani	Gs2,800
Peru	new sol	3.4 new sol
Philippines	peso	40 pesos
Poland	zloty	35,000 zlotys
Portugal	escudo	Es250
Puerto Rico	US dollar	$1.5*
Qatar	riyal	QR5.7
Romania	leu, lei	2,600 lei
Russia	rouble	Rbs‡
Rwanda	franc	RwFr220
St Lucia	E. Caribbean $	EC$4.2
St Vincent	E. Caribbean $	EC$4.2
San Marino	Italian lira	L2,400
Sao Tome	dobra	1,100 dobras
Saudi Arabia	riyal	SR5.8
Senegal	CFA franc	CFA Fr830
Seychelles	rupee	SRs7.6
Sierra Leone	leone	900 leone
Singapore	Singapore dollar	S$2.3
Slovakia	koruna	Kcs48
Slovenia	tolar	T200
Solomon Islands	dollar	SI$5
Somalia	shilling	SoSh4,000
South Africa	rand	R5.7
Spain	peseta	Pta200
Sri Lanka	rupee	SLRs75
Sudan	dinar	SD48

Surinam	Surinam guilder	SFl 285
Swaziland	lilangeni	5.7 lilangeni
Sweden	krona, kronor	SKr12
Switzerland	Swiss franc	SFr2.1
Syria	Syrian pound	S£32
Taiwan	Taiwan dollar	T$41
Tajikistan	rouble	Rbs‡
Tanzania	shilling	TSh800
Thailand	baht	Bt39
Togo	CFA franc	CFA Fr830
Tonga	pa'anga	T$2.0
Trinidad/Tobago	TT dollar	TT$8.7
Tunisia	dinar	TD1.5
Turkey	lira	TL50,000
Turkmenistan	manat	‡
Uganda	new shilling	USh1,500
UAE	dirham	Dh5.7
Ukraine	karbovanets	‡
United States	dollar	$1.5
Uruguay	peso Uruguayo	8 pesos
Uzbekistan	coupon	‡
Vanuatu	vatu	Vt175
Venezuela	bolivar	260 bolivars
Vietnam	dong	17,000 dong
Virgin Islands	US dollar	$1.5*
Western Samoa	taia	3.9 taias
Yemen (North)	rial	YR90
Yemen (South)	dinar	YD0.68
Yugoslavia†	new dinar	ND‡
Zaire	zaire	Z1,200
Zambia	kwacha	K1,050
Zimbabwe	Zimbabwe dollar	Z$12

†Rump Yugoslavia is Serbia and Montenegro.

Fractions
Examples: **£1.50, DM6.20, $38.16; 33p, 16 cents**.
An exception is the London market in gilt-edged securities where fractions of a pound are used.

SDRs, Ecus
These are currency cocktails which are accounting units devised to minimise the effect of the fluctuation of individual exchange rates. Best known are the **Special Drawing Rights (SDR)**, used by the IMF, and the **European Currency Unit (Ecu)**, used by the EC. They should be converted to sterling or dollars at first mention.

ENERGY TERMS GLOSSARY

accommodation platform a platform adapted to provide living quarters for offshore workers. *See* **drilling platform**.

American Petroleum Institute organisation responsible for the API system of rating crude oils according to their specific gravity and purity.

barrel liquid volume measure equal to 42 US gallons or 35 imperial gallons; 1 tonne of oil is 7.33 barrels. Oil output should be expressed as **barrels a day (b/d)**.

barrel of oil equivalent (boe) oil plus gas measured by energy value as if it were all oil.

benzene an important raw material derived from petroleum.

blow-out an escape of oil or gas (usually accidental) from a well during drilling.

Brent crude a benchmark price for North Sea oil; Brent is the largest oil-field in the North Sea.

buy-back crude oil in some countries the host government reserves for itself a proportion of oil production. The producing companies can often buy this **buy-back crude** from the government at a **buy-back price**. Where the concession is owned jointly by host government and company, the crude oil belonging to the company is known as **equity crude**.

catalyst a substance that increases the rate of a chemical reaction without itself suffering any chemical change.

concession permission for a company to explore and develop a specific area for a specific time.

condensate field a gas reservoir in which part of the gas will readily condense into a liquid; condensates are a very light oil used as refinery and petrochemical feedstocks.

core a cylindrical sample of rock obtained when drilling for oil or gas.

crude oil oil produced after any associated gas has been removed; **heavy crude** has a higher proportion of heavier sulphur, making it more expensive to refine; **light crude** is a higher quality of crude containing less sulphur and is especially suitable for gasoline production.

Derv stands for **Diesel Engine Road Vehicle fuel**; a British name for diesel fuel.

drilling platform/rig a platform for carrying out offshore exploration and development, but without any processing facilities.

ethane a colourless, odourless, flammable gas obtained from natural gas and petroleum and used in the manufacture of organic chemicals.

gas oil a petroleum distillate intermediate between kerosene and light lubricating oil; used as a fuel and for heating.

gasoline the US name for petrol.

hydrocarbons compounds consisting wholly of hydrogen and carbon which form the bulk of oil and natural gas.

kerosene another name for paraffin; a light distillate used for lighting and heating and to provide aircraft fuel.

liquefied natural gas (LNG) natural gas which has been turned into a liquid for easier handling.

liquefied petroleum gas (LPG) mainly propane and butane; light hydrocarbon material held in liquid form.

methane a colourless, odourless, flammable gas, the principal constituent of natural gas.

naphtha an oil product from which chemicals such as ethylene can be extracted.

natural gas naturally occurring hydrocarbons produced as a gas, predominantly methane. Gas production is measured in cubic metres or cubic feet a day.

Organisation of Petroleum Exporting Countries (Opec) members are: Algeria, Ecuador, Gabon, Indonesia, Iran, Iraq, Kuwait, Libya, Nigeria, Qatar, Saudi Arabia, UAE, Venezuela. Based in Vienna.

participation crude a government's share of crude output in a joint venture with a production company, usually in return for the granting of development rights.

petrodollar money, paid in dollars, earned by a country for exporting petroleum.

petroleum thick, flammable crude oil consisting mainly of hydrocarbons; distillation separates it into petrol, paraffin, diesel oil, lubricating oil, etc.

production platform an offshore platform for the drilling of development wells and which carries processing plant to maintain a field in production.

propane a colourless, flammable gas found in petroleum and used as a fuel.

reserves that are already located and known to be economically recoverable are **proven reserves**; oil or gas that is known to exist and to be economically recoverable is **recoverable reserves**.

rig *see* **drilling platform**.

semi-submersible rig a floating drilling platform supported by underwater pontoons.

terminal an onshore installation capable of receiving oil or gas from a pipeline or tankers; not a refinery.

wildcat a speculative well drilled in the hope of finding oil or gas.

FINANCIAL AND MARKETS GLOSSARY

Note: Most terms should be defined on first mention in the non-specialist pages.

Accounting Standards Board (ASB) UK body that sets accounting standards. A subsidiary body of the **Financial Reporting Council**.

administrative receiver insolvency practitioner appointed when a company goes into receivership. If a company is unsalvageable, it may go straight to administrative receivership, presided over by an **administrative receiver**, usually known simply as the **receiver**.

advance corporation tax (ACT) early instalment of UK Corporation Tax, required under UK tax regime. It forms a minimum tax on companies which earn most of their profits overseas.

American Depositary Receipt (ADR) certificate issued by US banks to facilitate trading in overseas stocks and shares. Note the spelling.

American Stock Exchange the less important of New York's two stock markets, dwarfed by the **New York Stock Exchange**. Sometimes abbreviated to **Amex**, which is also a common abbreviation for American Express. To avoid confusion, Amex is best avoided in both senses.

antitrust laws US legislation to prevent monopolies and restraint of trade.

APR means annual percentage rate: the true rate of paying interest on a loan.

arbitrage taking advantage of small price differences (of securities or goods) in different markets to make a profit. It involves buying something to sell in another market or at another time.

arbitrageur traditionally someone who indulges in arbitrage of any sort; now a Wall Street term for a professional investor who specialises in issues during takeovers; do not use "arb" as an abbreviation.

asset stripping buying a business and then realising a profit by selling off the assets separately.

assets **fixed assets** are land, machines, factories; **current assets** consist of cash, money owed, stock, investments, work in progress; **intangible assets** are goodwill, trade marks, patents, etc; **liquid assets** are funds kept in cash or in a form that can be quickly and easily turned into cash.

balance of payments a statement of a country's net financial transactions with other countries. **Current account** measures balance of imports and exports and payments and receipts for services such as shipping, banking and tourism. **Capital account** measures movements of capital (bank deposits, securities, shares, property).

Bank for International Settlements (BIS) is the central bankers' bank and is based in Basle, Switzerland.

bankruptcy is insolvency procedure for individuals.

base rate the annual interest rate on which lending charges are calculated by British banks.

basis point usually one hundredth of a percentage point (0.01 per cent), used in quoting movements in interest rates or yields on securities. Define the term except on the markets or currency pages.

Basle committee committee set up by the **Bank for International Settlements** and based in Basle. It drew up international capital adequacy standards for banks and was once known as the **Cooke Committee**, after a former chairman, but this name should now be avoided.

bear an investor who expects share prices to fall. He sells shares (often those he does not possess) in the hope that prices will fall and he can buy them back more cheaply later. More generally, a pessimist about the market outlook. *See also* **bull**.

bear market a period of falling share prices; a pessimistic state of affairs. *See also* **bull market**.

bearer stocks stock not registered in the name of an owner, who can thus remain anonymous. Common on the continent of Europe.

bed and breakfast overnight tax-related share deal involving two clearly separate transactions in the same share, a sale in the evening and a repurchase on the following day. The deal is intended to establish a tax loss benefit.

Big Bang the changes in UK stock exchange practices that took place in 1986. They permitted institutions such as banks and insurance companies to own stock exchange subsidiaries, abolished the segregation between brokers and jobbers and ended the system of fixed commissions.

Big Board the New York Stock Exchange price display. A colloquialism best avoided.

Big Four in the UK the four large clearing banks: **Barclays**, **Midland**, **Lloyds** and **National Westminster**. In Japan the largest securities houses: **Daiwa**, **Nikko**, **Nomura** and **Yamaichi**.

Big Six the six big accountancy firms: **KPMG Peat Marwick**, **Price Waterhouse**, **Ernst & Young**, **Touche Ross**, **Coopers & Lybrand**, **Arthur Andersen**. Note spelling, absence of hyphens, presence of ampersands. Individual country arms of these groups may have slightly different names; where the local name is significantly different, the worldwide name should also be cited.

BIS ratio *see* **capital adequacy**.

blue chip a stock considered reliable with regard to dividend income and capital value.

bond a certificate of debt issued to raise funds. It normally has a fixed rate of interest and is repayable at a fixed date.

bond ratings gradings by debt rating agencies such as Standard and Poor's or Moody's to classify the investment-worthiness of a company's debt.

bought deal an arrangement where a broker buys all of a new issue of shares and sells them on to investors at a small premium.

Brady bonds securities issued by developing countries which have reached debt restructuring agreements with their foreign bank creditors; the bonds are backed in part by US Treasury bonds. They were introduced by James Brady during his time as US Treasury secretary.

Bretton Woods the site in New Hampshire, US, of an international conference in 1944 which resulted in the establishment of the World Bank and the International Monetary Fund.

Brown Book the Brown Book's official title is *Development of the Oil and Gas Resources of the United Kingdom*; an annual report.

budget deficit usually the gap between government spending and revenue and thus the amount that needs to be borrowed. Definition varies between countries. *See also* **public sector borrowing requirement.**

building society UK savings institution that specialises in loans for house purchase. Building societies are owned by their members.

bull an investor who expects share prices to rise. *See also* **bear.**

bull market a period of rising share prices; an optimistic state of affairs. *See also* **bear market.**

Bundesbank the German central bank.

buy-out/in *see* **management buy-out/in.**

Cable the London dollar/sterling foreign exchange market. Outdated but still used by insiders. Avoid.

capital the money a company has to invest in buildings, machinery, etc; **equity capital** is that part of the capital subscribed by shareholders; **loan capital** is what the company has borrowed; **reserves** is money that the company has retained from its earnings.

capital adequacy a measure of the financial strength of a bank or securities firm, usually expressed as a ratio of its capital to its assets. For banks, there is now a worldwide capital adequacy standard, drawn up by the **Basle committee**, *qv*, of the **Bank for International Settlements.** This BIS ratio requires banks to have capital equal to 8 per cent of their assets.

capital gain the profit made on the sale of shares, commodities or land; **capital gains tax** is payable on the profit.

capital market place where securities such as shares, bonds, stocks are traded and where new securities can be issued. Usually used when referring to the issuing of medium and long-term finance.

cash flow pre-tax profits plus depreciation allowances and other charges.

certificate of deposit (CD) interest-bearing certificate issued by a bank to a large depositor. Especially common in the US.

central bank the major regulatory bank in a country, usually government controlled. Write, for example, **the Swiss central bank**, without initial capitals (except the Irish **Central Bank**, which is its name). The UK central bank is the **Bank of England**; Germany's is the **Bundesbank**; in the US it is the **Federal Reserve System (Fed)** *qv*.

Chapter 11 in the US a company can file for protection under Chapter 11 of the country's bankruptcy laws. The company continues to operate under existing management while working with its creditors to reorganise the business. Note that there are different Chapters, with different implications, though we usually write about Chapter 11.

churning occurs when sales agents urge a client to cash in an existing insurance policy after a short time and replace it with another. It is a lucrative practice because agents earn commission on each new policy they sell. It is also illegal.

City, the normally means the financial community in the City of London. In the FT International Edition this should be made quite clear.

clearing bank member bank of a national cheque clearing system. In England the clearing banks are **Barclays, Coutts, Lloyds, Midland** and **National Westminster**. In Scotland **The Bank of Scotland, Clydesdale Bank** and **The Royal Bank of Scotland**. Changing conditions make this an increasingly archaic term, best avoided.

clearing house interbank payment system (Chips) a computerised payment system for clearing cheques in New York.

clearing house automated payment system (Chaps) a computerised payment system for clearing cheques in the UK.

commercial paper short-term securities (typically 90 days in maturity) issued by companies to raise working capital.

compulsory liquidation liquidation of a company brought about by a court order, usually as the result of a petition by an unpaid creditor.

consortium bank a bank jointly owned by a number of other banks. An increasingly unfashionable way for small banks to engage in eurocurrency business.

consumer price index (CPI) a measure of the change in the cost of consumer goods and services. It is used as an indicator of a nation's inflation rate.

convertible bond a bond that can be converted into shares of the issuing company or its parent.

convertible currency a currency whose monetary authority allows holders to switch freely into other currencies or gold.

coupon literally a small certificate which is detachable from a bond to be exchanged for dividends, interest payments, etc. Also used to mean the rate of interest payable on a fixed-interest security.

credit ratings *see* **debt ratings**.

cross rate the exchange rate between two currencies. other than those that form a market's principal rates. Thus, in London, the D-Mark/franc rate is a cross rate.

cum *see* **ex**.

currency swap two parties exchange specific amounts of two different currencies and repay over time, payments being based on fixed interest rates in each currency.

current cost accounting a system designed to adjust accounting for changes in prices that affect a company's assets. The more usual convention is **historical cost accounting**.

debenture a long-term corporate bond, bearing fixed interest and often unsecured, issued by a company or government agency; assets may be pledged as security.

debt ratings triple A is the top rating for creditworthiness of a borrower as measured in the US by debt rating agencies **Moody's** and **Standard & Poor's**. A triple A rating means that there is almost no likelihood of the borrower failing to pay. Ratings should be written out: **triple A** (not **AAA**); **double B minus** (not **BB-**).

debt refinancing involves raising new money to repay existing debt. It is something borrowers do all the time, and should not be confused with **debt restructuring**, a more fundamental process in which a borrower changes the structure of its debts (this usually happens when a borrower gets into trouble, and involves a reorganisation of its liabilities, for instance by converting debt into equity). **Debt rescheduling** refers to a delay in the repayment of a debt, usually applying to both interest and principal payments, and can involve a renegotiation of the terms of the debt.

depreciation writing down the value of an asset in a company's books to reflect its loss of value through age and use.

derivatives futures and options contracts.

discount house company that specialises in discounting bills of exchange, Treasury bills and short-dated government bonds. The Bank of England uses discount houses to counteract shortages of day-to-day credit.

discount rate in the US the rate at which the **Federal Reserve**, *qv*, will lend short-term funds. Most countries' bank rates are known as the **discount rate**.

disqualification in the UK a director found guilty of "unfit" conduct may be disqualified from holding any management position for between 2 and 15 years; around 300–400 such orders are made each year.

dividend the amount a company distributes per share to shareholders. Failure to pay is know as **passing**, a heinous crime in the UK but more common elsewhere. UK dividends are usually paid twice a year; US dividends are paid quarterly.

dividend cover the number of times a company's most recent net dividend to shareholders could be paid out of its annual earnings (profits after tax).

earnings the amount of profit available to ordinary shareholders: that is, the profit after all operating expenses, interest charges, taxes and dividends on preference stock, but excluding extraordinary items. It is often expressed as **earnings per share**: the year's earnings divided by the number of ordinary shares. In the UK, do not confuse with **profit**, *qv*. (In the US earnings is often used interchangeably with profit.)

economic and monetary union (Emu) the European Community's plans for economic and monetary convergence among member countries, culminating in the introduction of a single currency.

electronic funds transfer at point of sale (Eftpos) for example using a plastic card in a shop's computer terminal, directly debiting the customer's bank account.

employee share ownership plan (Esop) a means for employees to acquire ownership of shares in their company without necessarily laying out personal capital. In the UK version shares are acquired through an **employee benefit trust (EBT)** and later distributed through an Inland Revenue approved **profit sharing trust (PST)**. Shares may be given or sold to employees.

endowment policy a combination of life assurance and investment whereby the sum assured is paid at a predetermined date or on death, if earlier.

equity a shareholder's equity is the value of shares s/he holds. A house owner's equity is the value of the house minus the unpaid mortgage. Thus **negative equity** occurs when the house is worth less than the debt on it.

eurobond a bond or note which usually has a final fixed maturity but occasionally is perpetual, issued in a **eurocurrency**, *qv*. The buyer of the bond usually holds it outside the country of origin of the currency in which it is denominated.

All **euro** prefixes are lower case and one word.

eurocurrency any currency held by banks, corporations or individuals outside its country of origin: eg, **eurodollar, eurosterling**, etc. The euro part of the name derives from the place where the first market in such currencies (normally dollars) arose.

euromarket the international capital markets that deal in eurobonds, etc.

European Monetary System (EMS) set up in 1979, the EMS now includes all EU currencies. These currencies determine the value of the Community's composite currency, the **European currency unit (Ecu)**, which is a basket weighted according to each country's share of EC output. All EC members except Greece have participated in the system's **exchange rate mechanism (ERM)**, which limits the amount by which currencies can fluctuate against each other.

ex dividend, **ex rights**, **ex cap**, **ex all** **ex div** means that the buyer of a share is not entitled to the next dividend payment (it appears as **xd** in share listings); **ex rights** not entitled to shares from a forthcoming rights issue; **ex cap** not entitled to a scrip issue; **ex all** not entitled to any of these. If the entitlement exists, the shares are **cum div, cum rights, cum cap, cum all**.

exchange rate mechanism (ERM) of the European Monetary System. An arrangement by which participating governments commit themselves to maintain the value of their currencies in relation to the European currency unit, taking action to correct any divergence from agreed limits.

face value the nominal value on the face of a certificate or bond; market value is often very different from face value.

factor an agent who carries out business for someone on a commission basis; often a sort of debt collector.

federal funds rate rate at which banks in the US lend reserves to each other. A key short-term money rate in New York, often influenced by the **Federal Reserve**, *qv*, injecting or withdrawing funds to control the price of money.

Federal National Mortgage Association (Fannie Mae) in the US, the government-backed residential mortgage agency.

Federal Reserve System (Fed) the central banking system of the US consisting of 12 **Federal Reserve Banks** controlling 12 districts under the control of the **Federal Reserve Board**.

Fimbra is the **Financial Intermediaries, Managers and Brokers Regulatory Association**, the self-regulatory organisation for independent financial advisers.

firm used in the FT for partnerships: accountants, stockbrokers, etc; and sometimes for small companies, privately owned. Otherwise write **company, concern, group, business**.

floating rate note (FRN) medium-term loan stock in a company which pays interest that varies according to money market conditions; they can be medium or long-term or perpetual.

forex is an abbreviation of **foreign exchange** and is best confined to the currencies and markets pages.

forward market a market in forward contracts of a commodity or currency, which are agreements to buy or sell the commodity or currency at a future date. The contracts are not negotiable.

front end loading of a loan or insurance policy occurs when all or most of the charges and commissions are imposed when the loan or policy is taken out. An insurer can then benefit by persuading the buyer to cash in a policy and take out a new one. *See also* **churning**

FT indices the **FT Index** is the **FT Ordinary Share Index**, also known as the **30 Share Index**. This started in 1935 at 100, and is based on the prices of 30 leading industrial and commercial shares. There are a number of other FT indices, including the **FT-SE 100 Index, the FT-A All-Share Index** and the **FT-A World Index**.
See **Stock market indices** on pages 221–224.

fund to fund is a technical term; do not use it to mean to finance.

futures contract a contract which requires the delivery of a commodity at a specified date, if not liquidated before that date. Futures markets exist for many commodities and currencies.

gearing a measure of the degree to which a business is funded by debt rather than shareholders' equity. The US expression for the same thing is **leverage**. A highly geared company carries a lot of debt.

gilt-edged securities securities with interest and repayment guaranteed by the British government. Often used as a synonym for high quality. Note: the securities are known as **gilts**, the market is the **gilt market** (singular not plural).

global custody a global custodian, usually a bank, makes sure that its clients' cross-border investments are safe and sound.

greenmail in the US, payment by a takeover target to a potential bidder, usually to buy back acquired shares at a premium in return for the predator not pursuing the bid.

grey market unofficial trading of securities before their formal issue.

gross domestic product (GDP) is the total value of all goods and services produced domestically each year by a country. It equals gross national product minus income from abroad. Most countries use this definition; US official statistics use gross national product.

gross national product (GNP) is the total value of goods and services produced each year by a country. Real growth in GNP measures the increase in output after subtracting the effect of inflation.

hedging insuring against price fluctuations by taking equal and opposite positions in two different markets, eg, in futures and cash markets.

holding company a company whose main assets are its shareholdings (usually controlling) in other companies. Note: UK holding companies often have names such as **HSBC Holdings**. Continental holding companies may be, for example, **CS Holding** (no s).

Imro is the **Investment Management Regulatory Organisation**, the regulatory organisation for investment companies such as pension funds.

index of leading economic indicators is compiled by the US Commerce Department and is a composite of 12 economic measurements.

inflation is a general increase in prices.

inheritance tax UK tax charged on the passing of wealth from one person to another, either during life or at death.

insider dealing or **trading** illegal exploitation of confidential information in order to make a profit or avoid a loss on market transactions.

insolvency occurs when individuals or businesses do not have enough resources to cover their debts, or cannot pay their debts when they are due.

institutional investor a large financial institution, such as an insurance company, pension fund, unit trust or investment trust.

insurance broker a specialised broker who secures insurance business and places it with recognised underwriters.

investment trust a company that invests a fixed amount of money in a variety of stocks and shares as a way of spreading risks. Investment trusts have fixed capital, unlike **unit trusts** which can create or redeem units in response to demand.

Investors' Compensation Scheme a statutory scheme operated by the Securities and Investment Board to give individual investors up to £48,000 protection if an authorised investment business collapses.

invisible income foreign income from sources other than the movement of goods; it includes earnings from tourism, banking, shipping, insurance and investment.

joint venture co-operation on a project between two or more companies or countries.

junk bonds high-yield bonds that are below investment grade (BAA by Moody's or triple B by Standard & Poor's) which are often used to fund takeovers and buy-outs.

Lautro is the **Life Assurance and Unit Trust Regulatory Organisation**. It is sufficient to write: **Lautro, the UK insurance industry's self-regulatory body** or **the self-regulating body for the UK insurance industry**. It should not be referred to unexplained.

leverage *see* **gearing**.

leveraged buy-out the raising of funds to buy out a company, the company's assets being used as collateral for the borrowing. The loans are repaid from the company's cash flow or by selling its assets. *See also* **management buy-out**.

liabilities the debts of a company and claims against it; the opposite of **assets**, *qv*.

Libid and **Libor** **Libid** is the **London interbank bid rate**, the rate that a bank is willing to pay for funds in the international interbank market; **Libor** is the **London interbank offered rate**, the rate at which banks offer to lend funds in this market. The average of the two is **Limean**. In practice, Libor is much the most frequently quoted.

life assurance assures the payment of agreed sums of money on a given date or on death, in return for the payment of regular premiums.

Liffe is the **London International Financial Futures Exchange**. The full name should appear early in a news story.

liquidation a process which brings a company's existence to an end after distributing its assets. A liquidator is the insolvency practitioner who winds up a company.

liquidity the proportion of cash in a company's assets; also assets that are easily capable of being turned into cash.

loan capital part of a company's capital made up of loans from outside the company. **Loan stock** is stock issued against loans, either **unsecured loan stock** or **debenture stock**; the latter is secured by a charge on assets.

Lombard rate is the rate at which the Bundesbank, the German central bank, lends funds to banks as short-term credit. It is normally at least 1 percentage point above the discount rate and is regarded as an important international indicator.

long investors are long if they have bought shares but not yet arranged an offsetting sale. *See also* **short**.

management buy-in purchase of a troubled company by investors who offer a new set of managers.

management buy-out the purchase of a company by its managers, usually with outside backing.

market capitalisation the value at current market prices of a company's equity capital. It equals the share price times the number of shares outstanding.

merchant bank a specialised bank offering investment services, corporate advice, trade and project finance, exchange rate dealing, etc, to clients worldwide. It also acts as an issuing house for stocks and bonds, and advises companies involved in mergers.

minimum lending rate the minimum rate of interest at which the Bank of England was willing to lend to the money market; discontinued in 1981, but occasionally reused in moments of crisis.

monetary compensatory amounts (MCAs) part of a complicated system of levies and subsidies designed to iron out currency-related distortions in EC cross-border farm trade.

money supply the total amount of money in an economy, as described by definitions **M0, M2, M4, M4c, M5**. The most widely used are: **M0**, the wide monetary base, which consists of notes and coins in circulation outside the Bank of England, plus bankers' operational deposits within the bank; and **M4**, which consists of the private sector's holdings of notes and coins and all sterling deposits at UK banks and building societies. In Germany **M3** includes cash in circulation, current accounts and short-term deposits.

multinational a company with subsidiaries or manufacturing bases in several overseas countries.

mutual fund US name for **unit trust**, *qv*.

Name wealthy individual whose capital backs the Lloyd's of London insurance market.

Nasdaq system The **National Association of Securities Dealers Automated Quotation** system, operated in the US by the National Association of

Securities Dealers. A computerised system for providing price quotes for securities in the US.

net profit strictly the profit of a company after deducting all prior charges including taxes, depreciation, auditors' and directors' fees.

New York Stock Exchange (NYSE) Wall Street is permissible in headings and summary columns. The colloquial use of **Big Board** for the exchange's display should be avoided.

official receiver in the UK a civil servant and also a court officer, attached to the **Insolvency Service**, which is an executive agency of the Department of Trade and Industry. The official receiver is first on the scene in any bankruptcy or compulsory liquidation.

offshore centre a financial centre free of many taxes and constraints, such as the Bahamas, Bahrain, Cayman Islands.

option an agreement entitling the holder to buy (**call**) or sell (**put**) shares or commodities, within a given time and at a given price, from or to the other party to the agreement.

ordinary shares rank after preference shares and debentures for dividend payments; the securities that usually confer ownership of the company. In the US they are known as **common stock**.

over-the-counter market (OTC) trading in shares away from organised exchanges; it is usually carried out over the telephone or via a computer network.

partly paid shares for which the buyer pays only part of the issue price initially, paying for the rest at predetermined dates, on the last of which they become **fully paid**.

personal equity plan (PEP) in the UK a plan that allows someone to invest a certain sum in equities each year without attracting income tax or capital gains tax. It is intended as a pension fund for people who otherwise do not contribute to one.

poison pill defensive tactics designed to fend off hostile takeovers.

pre-emptive rights give existing shareholders the right to buy additional shares in a new issue before it is offered to the public.

preference shares/preferred stock fixed dividend shares that rank above ordinary shares if a company is wound up.

price/earnings ratio a share's price divided by its last published earnings. It is used as a measure of whether a company's share should be considered expensive. Do not confuse with the **yield**, which is the dividend as a percentage of the share price. A **prospective p/e ratio** is based on the forecast of the next annual earnings to be published. A p/e is sometimes called a **multiple**.

prime rate the interest rate charged by US banks on loans to their most creditworthy borrowers; the benchmark for other interest rates.

private placement in the US is the sale of shares directly to an institutional investor rather than placing them on the market. The shares need not be registered with the Securities and Exchange Commission.

profit the excess of revenue over expenses relating to a particular period. Figures may be quoted as **gross profit**, **net profit before tax**, **net profit after tax** or **earnings**, *qv*. **Profit**, **trading profit** and **operating profit** all refer to the profit before interest and tax.

programme trading a batch of deals involving a number of different shares carried out simultaneously by a single stock market trader, who may either be acting for a client or have taken the programme on his own account. Many variations exist, including trading between stock index futures and equities and computer-triggered programme deals, which automatically buy or sell at preset prices.

public sector borrowing requirement (PSBR) in the UK the PSBR defines the amount that the public sector as a whole has to borrow in any financial year.

purchasing power parity method of valuation states that the correct exchange rate between two currencies is the one that equalises the price of the same traded item in both countries.

qualified audit report an auditor's report that says a company's financial statement gives a true and fair view subject to certain qualifying remarks. Companies try hard to avoid a qualification, which indicates weaknesses in their financial position or internal controls.

receiver *see* **administrative receiver; official receiver**.

reinsurance a **reinsurer** is an insurance company that helps to spread risks by accepting business from other insurance companies and underwriters.

reserves various categories of liquid assets of a bank or company consisting mainly of retained profits.

reserve currency an internationally acceptable currency which is held by other countries as part of their central reserves.

reserve requirement the proportion of deposits that a bank must by law keep in cash or place with the central bank.

retail banking banking services primarily for individuals and small businesses; **wholesale banking** deals with institutions and commercial concerns.

retail price index (RPI) a measure of the level of shop prices for goods. The **inflation rate** is the RPI's percentage increase usually compared with the same month the previous year. In the US the **consumer price index** does a similar job.

revolving credit a line of credit for a fixed sum, allowing repeated use of the credit providing that the fixed sum is not exceeded; regular scheduled repayments of predetermined amounts are made.

rights issue an offer of shares to existing shareholders usually at a discount to market price.

samurai bond a bond issued by a foreign borrower in Japan; denominated in yen, it can be bought by non-residents of Japan.

savings and loan (S&L) the US equivalent of a **building society**, providing funds for house purchase. Otherwise known as a **thrift**.

scrip issue or **capitalisation issue** or **bonus issue** an issue of shares to shareholders without payment; a way for a company to transfer money from reserves to permanent capital.

secondary market the buying and selling of existing stocks, shares, bonds, etc. New securities are placed in the **primary market**.

securities certificates or bearer warrants for stock, shares or bonds.

Securities and Exchange Commission (SEC) an official US body which regulates the securities industry.

Securities and Futures Authority (SFA) is the regulatory authority for securities and futures brokers in the UK. It handles complaints against stockbrokers. It was formed through a merger in 1991 of the Securities Association and the Association of Futures Brokers and Dealers.

Securities and Investment Board (SIB) a UK regulatory body set up in 1986 to oversee the investment business.

self-regulating organisations (SRO) are the four self-regulatory authorities in the UK: **Fimbra**, **Lautro**, **Imro**, **SFA**, *qv*.

short investors are **short** of a share or commodity if they have sold shares they do not possess, in the hope of buying them later at a lower price. *See also* **long**.

special deposits a proportion of a bank's assets that the Bank of England can require the bank to place on reserve with it.

spot market a market in goods or securities for immediate delivery.

Special Drawing Right (SDR) an international reserve asset created by the IMF in 1969 and used by it for book-keeping purposes. The SDR currency basket consists of the five weighted currencies of the G5 countries (dollar, D-Mark, pound, French franc and yen). Note that the value of the SDR quoted in the currency rates table on the FT currencies page is a rate; to convert to other currencies you multiply rather than divide.

spread a **yield spread** represents the differential between the yields on two comparable bonds in different markets. It can also be used to describe the differential between the yields on a eurobond and a comparable government bond of the same currency. If the spread **tightens**, this means the differential has narrowed, and if it **widens**, it has got bigger. If the spread on a bond tightens, this could mean that the bond is in demand, and if it widens this could mean the bond is not doing so well. (When the price of a bond rises, the yield falls and vice versa.)

A **bid/offer spread** is the difference between the price at which a market-maker or dealer is prepared to sell a share, bond, commodity or any other tradeable instrument, and the one at which s/he is prepared to buy. In the stock market, these spreads are shown on Seaq screens and the most advantageous bid and offer prices are displayed on the yellow strip at the top of the screen, known as the "touch".

stag someone who subscribes for a new issue in the hope of selling at a profit immediately dealing starts. Easy under a Conservative government which undervalued its utilities when privatising them.

stock split division of shares into a larger number of shares of lower unit value. Proportional ownership of the shares remains the same.

stockbroker person or firm undertaking to arrange the sale or purchase of shares or other securities for an institution or member of the public.

stocklending a legal and common practice whereby pension funds lend out their assets for a few days or weeks to other financial institutions as a way of boosting their income. Stocklending was used illegally by Robert Maxwell to divert money from pension funds to his private companies.

stop order an order for a broker to buy or sell shares or commodities when the price reaches a certain level.

swap the exchange of a stream of payments over time agreed by two counterparties; normally used to transform market exposure from one interest rate base to another or one currency to another. *See also* **currency swap**.

tap stock British government bond used to control the gilts market. Supplies may be turned on or off, hence the name; only a proportion is issued initially, the remainder being fed into the market by the government broker.

thrift *see* **savings and loan**.

times covered the number of times a company's profits can be divided by its dividend.

Treasury bill/bond/note notes issued by governments to finance short-term expenditure; in the UK normally for 91 days, in the US for 3 or 6 months. In the US, auctions of these bonds take place weekly (the **weekly tender**), their yields giving clues to interest rate trends.

trustee investment an investment in which trustees are authorised to invest money in a trust fund. A trustee holds title to a property on behalf of another.

trustee savings bank a bank managed by a body of trustees but which has most of the features of a clearing bank. Note: the former Trustee Savings Banks have now been transformed into **TSB Group**, with **TSB Bank** as its principal subsidiary. The words Trustee and Savings have disappeared.

underwriter a principal who underwrites an insurance policy; also someone who guarantees to buy up shares or bonds from an issue that are not taken up by the public.

unit trust a fund of stocks and shares held by a trustee for the benefit of subscribing investors; an easy means of obtaining a spread of investments. The British equivalent of a **mutual fund**.

unlisted securities market (USM) a market in small company shares administered by the stock exchange in the UK. A company cannot be listed on the USM but can be quoted or its shares traded on the USM. To be abolished.

voluntary liquidation a liquidation initiated by a company, not one imposed by a court.

Wall Street the financial district of New York in lower Manhattan; the American equivalent of the City of London. It can be used as a synonym for the US financial markets.

white knight someone who rescues a takeover target from an unwanted bidder.

winding up order an order made by a court for a company to be placed in compulsory liquidation.

window dressing efforts by companies to put a favourable gloss on their accounts, sometimes by raising short-term funds.

withholding tax tax deducted from dividends in the US, Canada and other countries when these are paid to non-residents. It can be reclaimed under certain conditions.

yield the rate of return on an investment. Also the dividend payable on a share expressed as a percentage of the market price. Although the FT quotes the net dividend (after basic rate tax), yields are calculated on a gross basis, ie assuming no tax is paid on the dividend.

LAW AND LIBEL

The imaginary litigant below is male, but could just as well be female; no slight is intended.

1. What is libel?

(a) Our law credits everyone, including a company, with a good reputation. If your story detracts from that reputation it is defamatory.

(b) Spot check test as to whether something is defamatory: how would you feel if it were said in your paper about you?

(c) If you are sued and cannot defend you have published a libel.

2. Identification

(a) Your readership must know whom you are talking about before someone can say he is libelled. Remember that a particular person has many identifying characteristics, of which the name is only one; for example, a photograph or association with a location or a cause. You can also libel a group if it is small enough. **One of the five directors ran off with the cash** may well bring you writs from at least four of them, even if you can prove the fifth did it.

(b) If reasonable readers acquainted with the person and with the circumstances described in your story recognise him, he is sufficiently identified and can sue.

3. Meanings

(a) A person has to show you have detracted from his reputation. You might think that the true meaning of your story does not detract from his reputation. But it is what you said that counts, not what you meant to say.

(b) If he can satisfy a jury that your story means what he says it means then he will probably win. You will not be equipped to defend a meaning you had not realised your story was capable of. Aim for precision: avoid ambiguities.

4. Will he complain?

(a) If you have done enough research and got your story right, you have the best possible shield against a libel action. Get his side of the story before you publish and use it.

(b) No one who cares about his reputation will take you to court if he realises you have published no more and no less than the truth about him.

(c) Make it clear in the story that you are sure of your facts and *never* depart from them in any way, whether it seems to you significant at the time or not.

5. Justification

(a) If you can prove it is true, you have a complete defence. You will very rarely need it because if it is true and he knows it is true he is not going to waste his time and yours with a libel action.

(b) Minor errors are theoretically irrelevant provided you can prove the substance of what you say. But in practice juries are merciless if they find there has been any colouring, unwarranted assumptions or sloppy research on facts.

(c) It is up to you to prove, not up to him to disprove. Proof is evidence sufficient to satisfy a jury that you are probably right. Off-the-record and non-attributable sources are no good for this purpose.

6. Fair comment

In commenting on your facts, do not let your opinions be influenced by any undeclared interest or motive but give your own honest views. Your opinions are then fair comment and your defence will not be defeated on the ground that you were "malicious". Avoid comment in news stories.

7. *Privilege*

(a) Generally, you can be called on to prove that what you have written is true. It is not enough to prove that you have heard someone else say it.

(b) In many cases, however, it is sufficient to prove that you heard someone else say it and that you have fairly and accurately reported what has been said or written by other people, whether it is true or not. This is the defence of privilege.

(c) Absolute privilege attaches to fair, accurate and contemporaneous newspaper reports of judicial proceedings in open court. Beware of reporting the start of a law case and then not giving both sides, or worse, of dropping it before a verdict is given. Watch for appeals. This is an important area. Equally important to you is the statutory qualified privilege conferred by Section 7 and the Schedule to the Defamation Act 1952. You should familiarise yourself with this. Qualified privilege attaches to fair and accurate reports of parliamentary proceedings

(d) Two golden rules: If you do not produce a fair and accurate report you lose the privilege. If anyone abuses an occasion of qualified privilege by sounding off in defamatory terms about something not to the point, he loses his privilege and so do you if you report him. You will lose qualified privilege if your decision to cover the event is influenced by any undeclared interest or motive.

(e) Section 7 extends to some matters outside the UK but not nearly as widely as is desirable.

(f) Reports from abroad under common law are covered by qualified privilege if the subject matter is of sufficient interest to readers in this country. What is of sufficient interest? It is for the court to say and your best course if in doubt is to take advice.

8. *Contempt*

There is no hard and fast rule, even after the Contempt of Court Act 1981. If your story prejudices or impedes the fair trial of an action in the courts it is in contempt. The closer the trial, the greater the danger. Ask yourself whether a jury member reading and believing your story might be prejudiced in favour of one side or the other. If so, take advice.

Watch out for postponement orders under Section 4(2) of the 1981 Act.

Have the list of things which can be mentioned in reports of committal and preparatory proceedings handy, in case of need. They are now in Section 8 of the Magistrates Courts Act 1980 and Section 11 of the Criminal Justice Act respectively. If you do not know whether reporting restrictions have been lifted, take advice.

There are many other reporting restrictions, notably in cases involving minors and rape cases, with which you should familiarise yourself.

Once a lawyer has approved a story, no further changes should be made without referring back.

Note: The above represents guidance on a principled approach to the subject of law and libel and does not profess to be a precis of the entire law.

MEASURES

Multiples

nano is a thousand millionth (a billionth)
micro is a millionth
milli is a thousandth
centi is a hundredth
deci is a tenth
deca is ten times
hecto is 100 times
kilo is 1,000 times
mega is 1 million times
giga is 1,000 million times
tera is a million million times

Note that a **billion** (**bn**) is 1,000 million and a **trillion** is 1 million million; try to avoid trillion if possible: **3 trillion = 3,000bn.**

Distance and area

Unit	*Abbreviation*
mile	3 miles
miles per hour	3mph
square mile	3 square miles
yard	3 yards
foot	3ft
square foot	3 sq ft
kilometre	3km
kilometres per hour	3km/h
square kilometre	3 sq km
metre	3m
square metre	3 sq m
centimetre	3cm
square centimetre	3 sq cm
millimetre	3mm
hectare	3ha
knot*	3 knots

*The knot is the nautical mile per hour = 1.15mph.

Volume

cubic foot	3 cu ft
cubic metre	3 cu m
cubic centimetres	3cc
gallon	3 gallons
litre	3 litres
centilitres	3cl
millilitres	3ml

Weight

ton	3 tons
hundredweight	3cwt
pound	3lb but 23p a pound
tonne (metric)	3 tonnes
kilogramme	3kg
gramme	3g

The **imperial ton** is a **long ton** (2,240lb). In the US the **short ton** of 2,000lb is used. To convert short tons into long, multiply by 0.89 (it is very unlikely that you will wish to do this). The long ton and the metric **tonne** are nearly identical. Tonne is most commonly used in stories about the UK, Europe, Asia and Australasia; ton where the US is concerned.

Bullion

Gold, silver and platinum are reckoned in troy weight, where one ounce is the equivalent of roughly 1 1/10 ounces avoirdupois. On the continent of Europe gold is traded in metric measure. 1 ounce troy = 31.1 grammes.

Map references

Degrees of latitude define the distance of a place north or south of the equator, degrees of longitude those east or west from the Greenwich meridian. Write as follows: **47deg 32'N, 32deg 47'E.**

32' means 32 minutes, ie 32/60 of a degree.

Ships

The size of passenger ships is expressed in **gross tonnage (grt)**, of tankers and bulk carriers in **deadweight tons (dwt)**, that of warships in **displacement tons**, of yachts in **Thames measurement**.

Energy

British thermal unit	10Btu
therm	20 therms
horsepower	10hp
joule	10 joules
watt	100W
kilowatt (W × 1,000)	10kW
megawatt (kW × 1,000)	10MW
gigawatt (MW × 1,000)	10GW or (preferably) 10,000MW

Oil

The oil industry in general measures quantities of oil in barrels, where one standard barrel equals 35 imperial gallons. There are 7.33 barrels of oil to 1 metric tonne, and 6.29 barrels to 1 cubic metre. Output is often measured in **barrels a day**, which at the second reference may be expressed as **b/d**; also in **boe, barrels of oil equivalent**.

Gas

The **joule** has replaced the therm and the British thermal unit as a measure of gas supply.

British Gas now measures domestic consumption in **kilowatt hours (kWh)** instead of therms. **1 therm = 29.3071kWh.**

Temperatures

Temperature is generally expressed in Celsius; Fahrenheit temperatures should have a Celsius conversion added in parentheses: **73°F (23°C)**.

Conversion Table

In the table below the left columns are Celsius, the right columns Fahrenheit.

45	113	30	86	15	59	0	32
44	111	29	84	14	57	-1	30
43	109	28	82	13	55	-2	28
42	108	27	81	12	54	-3	27
41	106	26	79	11	52	-4	25
40	104	25	77	10	50	-5	23
39	102	24	75	9	48	-6	21
38	100	23	73	8	46	-7	19
37	99	22	72	7	45	-8	18
36	97	21	70	6	43	-9	16
35	95	20	68	5	41	-10	14
34	93	19	66	4	39	-11	12
33	91	18	64	3	37	-12	10
32	90	17	63	2	36		
31	88	16	61	1	34		

Some conversion factors

To convert, multiply by the relevant number.

Unit	Metric into imperial	Imperial into metric	Unit
km	0.621	1.61	miles
metres	1.09	0.91	yards
cm	0.39	2.54	inches
sq km	0.39	2.59	sq miles
hectares	2.47	0.40	acres
sq metres	10.76	0.09	sq feet
sq metres	1.196	0.836	sq yards
sq cm	0.16	6.45	sq inches
cu metres	35.3	0.03	cu feet
cu cm	0.06	16.39	cu inches
litres	1.76	0.57	pints
litres	0.22	4.546	gallon
kilogramme	2.2	0.45	lb
grammes	0.04	28.35	ounces
litres/100km	0.355	2.82	gallon/miles

km/litre	2.82	0.355	miles/gallon
kilojoules	0.947	1.055	Btu
kilowatts	1.33	0.75	horsepower
kilowatt hours	0.034	29.3071	therms
litres	0.0063	159	barrels (oil)

Approximate conversions

1 inch	2½ centimetres
1 foot	30 centimetres
1 metre	39 inches
8 kilometres	5 miles
6 square yards	5 square metres
1 hectare	2½ acres
1 square kilometre	250 acres
1 pint	568 millilitres
1 litre	1¾ pints
1 gallon (UK)	4½ litres
5 gallons (UK)	6 gallons (US)
1 cubic metre	35 cubic feet
3 cubic metres	4 cubic yards
1 barrel (petroleum)	35 gallons (UK)
1 barrel a day	50 tonnes a year
4 horsepower (UK)	3 kilowatts
1 grain	65 milligrammes
1 gramme	15½ grains
1 ounce	28 grammes
1 troy ounce	31 grammes
1 pound	454 grammes
1 kilogram	2¼ pounds
1 tonne	2,205 pounds
50 miles an hour	80 kilometres an hour
20 miles per gallon (UK)	7 kilometres per litre
20 miles per gallon (UK)	14 litres per 100 kilometres

NUCLEAR TERMS GLOSSARY

advanced gas-cooled reactor (AGR) a distinctively British reactor design, developed as the second UK generation of commercial nuclear power stations. Seven AGRs were commissioned during the 1970s and 1980s (seven in England and two in Scotland) but the UK nuclear industry sees the design in retrospect as a mistake, because it is more expensive to build and operate than the **PWR**.

core the assembly of nuclear fuel (enriched uranium and/or plutonium) whose **fission** is the energy source for a reactor.

fast reactor a reactor in which fast **neutrons** sustain the nuclear chain reaction. The process breeds new nuclear fuel because surplus neutrons convert the non-fissile **isotope** uranium-238 into fissile plutonium (*see* **fission**). Prototype fast reactors have operated for many years in several countries (the UK example is at Dounreay on the north coast of Scotland) but, with conventional nuclear fuel expected to remain cheap for decades to come, the economics of the industry do not favour their commercial development at present.

fission the disintegration of a fissile heavy atom into two or more lighter ones (the fission products). The energy released by this process drives all today's nuclear reactors.

fusion the joining of two light atoms into a heavier one, the opposite process to **fission**. The energy released powers the sun and stars – and the hydrogen bomb – but has not yet been tamed for use in a nuclear power station. Fusion experiments such as the Joint European Torus (Jet) in Oxfordshire have shown promise but commercial fusion reactors are unlikely to enter service before the year 2040.

isotopes forms of a chemical element with different atomic masses, resulting from the presence of different numbers of neutrons. The most important isotope for nuclear power is uranium-235.

Magnox the design of the Britain's first generation of commercial reactors. (The name comes from the magnesium alloy used as fuel cladding in Magnox reactors.) Eleven Magnox plants were commissioned between 1956 (Calder Hall) and 1971 (Wylfa). Most are still running in the 1990s.

pressurised water reactor (PWR) The most widely used international design of commercial reactor. Nuclear Electric is building the UK's first PWR, Sizewell B, on the Suffolk coast.

radiation energy travelling in the form of electromagnetic rays or sub-atomic particles. In the nuclear industry, the term is normally taken to mean ionising radiation – radiation with sufficient energy to produce ions by knocking electrons off atoms in its path – as opposed to non-ionising radiation such as ordinary light. Large doses of ionising radiation are harmful to living tissues and may induce leukaemia and other cancers.

radioactivity spontaneous fission of unstable atoms, accompanied by the release of radiation.

reprocessing the separation of spent nuclear fuel into plutonium and uranium – which can be reused – and radioactive waste products.

ORGANISATIONS AND GROUPINGS

Amnesty International
The human rights organisation: do not write British-based, although its secretariat is in London.

Asia Pacific Economic Co-operation (Apec)
An economic and trade forum initiated by Australia in 1989. It includes the US, Canada, Australia, Japan, China, Hong Kong, Taiwan and the Asean nations. Secretariat in Singapore.

Association of South East Asian Nations (Asean)
Brunei, Indonesia, Malaysia, the Philippines, Singapore and Thailand. A body which aims to promote social, economic and cultural progess in its member states. Founded in 1967. Headquarters is in Jakarta, Indonesia.

Asian Development Bank
The ADB aims to promote economic and social development of its member countries. Members are 32 countries from the Asia-Pacific region and 15 from Europe and North America. Based in Manila, Philippines.

Bank for International Settlements (BIS)
The BIS is based in Basle, Switzerland, and acts as a banker to central banks. It provides facilities for international financial operations, including the clearing operations for the European Monetary System.

Caribbean Community and Common Market (Caricom)
Members are Antigua and Barbuda, Bahamas (not a member of the Common Market), Barbados, Belize, Dominica, Grenada, Guyana, Jamaica, Montserrat, St Kitts-Nevis, St Lucia, St Vincent and the Grenadines, Trinidad and Tobago. The British Virgin Islands and the Turks and Caicos Islands are associate members. Headquarters is in Georgetown, Guyana.

Cern (European Organisation for Nuclear Research)
Cern promotes European collaboration in nuclear research for peaceful purposes. It has 19 member countries. Headquarters in Geneva.

Club du Sahel

A multilateral donor organisation whose members are the 22 countries of the **Sahel** region of sub-Saharan Africa. The **United Nations Sudano-Sahelian office** provides aid and co-ordinates relief work in the area.

Co-ordinating Committee for Multilateral Export Controls (Cocom)

Cocom was set up in 1949 to prevent the export of advanced technology from industrial countries to communist states. Members are Nato members (minus Iceland) plus Japan and Australia. Headquarters were in Paris. Cocom was disbanded on March 31 1994.

Comecon

Formerly the Council for Mutual Economic Assistance, the communist world's version of the EC; disbanded in June 1991. (Members were Bulgaria, Cuba, Czechoslovakia, East Germany, Hungary, Poland, Romania, Soviet Union, Vietnam.)

Commonwealth

Members are: Antigua and Barbuda, Australia, Bahamas, Bangladesh, Barbados, Belize, Botswana, Brunei, Canada, Cyprus, Dominica, the Gambia, Ghana, Grenada, Guyana, India, Jamaica, Kenya, Kiribati, Lesotho, Malawi, Malaysia, the Maldives, Malta, Mauritius, Namibia, Nauru, New Zealand, Nigeria, Pakistan, Papua New Guinea, St Kitts-Nevis, St Lucia, St Vincent and the Grenadines, Seychelles, Sierra Leone, Singapore, Solomon Islands, Sri Lanka, Swaziland, Tanzania, Tonga, Trinidad and Tobago, Tuvalu, Uganda, United Kingdom, Vanuatu, Western Samoa, Zambia, Zimbabwe.

Pakistan left the Commonwealth in 1972 but rejoined in 1989; South Africa left in 1961 and rejoined in 1994; Fiji left in 1987.

Conference on Security and Co-operation in Europe (CSCE)

A forum designed to build on east-west agreements reached in Helsinki in 1975. Later conferences were held in Belgrade (1977–80), Madrid (1980–83), Vienna (1986–89) and Helsinki (1992). The conference's present aim is to provide a security framework for Europe. Members are Albania, Armenia, Austria, Azerbaijan, Belarus, Belgium, Bosnia-Hercegovina, Bulgaria, Canada, Croatia, Cyprus, Czech Republic, Denmark, Estonia, Finland, France, Georgia, Germany, Greece, Hungary, Iceland, Ireland, Italy, Kazakhstan, Kyrgyzstan, Latvia, Liechtenstein, Lithuania, Luxembourg,

Malta, Moldova, Monaco, the Netherlands, Norway, Poland, Portugal, Romania, the Russian Federation, San Marino, Slovakia, Slovenia, Spain, Sweden, Switzerland, Tajikistan, Turkey, Turkmenistan, UK, Ukraine, USA, Uzbekistan, the Vatican, Yugoslavia. The secretariat is in Prague, a Conflict Prevention Centre in Vienna and an Office for Democratic Insititutions and Human Rights in Warsaw.

Council of Europe

Aims to achieve greater unity and promote economic and social progress among its member countries. Members are Austria, Belgium, Bulgaria, Cyprus, Czech Republic, Denmark, Estonia, Finland, France, Germany, Greece, Hungary, Iceland, Ireland, Italy, Liechtenstein, Lithuania, Luxembourg, Malta, Netherlands, Norway, Poland, Portugal, San Marino, Slovakia, Slovenia, Spain, Sweden, Switzerland, Turkey, UK. Special guest status is held by Albania, Croatia, Estonia, Latvia, Lithuania, Romania, the Russian Federation and Slovenia. Headquarters in Strasbourg, France.

Council of Ministers

The Council of the European Communities consists of ministers from each of the 12 EU member countries. Which ministers depends on the subject under discussion. It is the main decision-taking body in the EU legislative process, acting on the basis of proposals by the **European Commission**, *qv*. The European Council consists of the heads of government of member states. The presidency of the EU, which is held in rotation for six month periods, sets the agenda for European Council meetings.

Portugal and the UK held the presidency in 1992; other holders are:

1993 Denmark, Belgium
1994 Greece, Germany
1995 France, Spain
1996 Italy, Ireland

Council headquarters is in Brussels.

Court of Auditors

An EC body which is responsible for the audit and financial management of EC resources. It has 12 members appointed by the Council of Ministers. Sited in Luxembourg.

Economic Community of West African States (Ecowas)
Ecowas aims to promote economic, social and cultural development of its member states. Members are: Benin, Burkina Faso, Cape Verde, the Gambia, Ghana, Guinea, Guinea-Bissau, Ivory Coast, Liberia, Mali, Mauritania, Niger, Nigeria, Senegal, Sierra Leone, Togo. Headquarters in Lagos, Nigeria.

European Atomic Energy Community (Euratom)
An organisation dedicated to producing nuclear energy for peaceful purposes on a large scale within the EC.

European Bank for Reconstruction and Development (EBRD)
An international bank set up in 1991 to help the economic and political regeneration of central and eastern Europe (Albania, Bulgaria, Czech Republic, Estonia, Hungary, Latvia, Lithuania, Poland, Romania, former Soviet Union, former Yugoslavia). Inaugurated on May 29 1991, its charter was signed by 40 countries. It now (1994) has 55 country members. The European Investment Bank of the European Community are also members. Headquarters in London.

European Commission
The Commission is the initiator of European Union action and acts as a mediator between governments in EU affairs; it is the guardian of the European Community and Union treaties. Its 17 commissioners are normally appointed for a four-year renewable term. There are currently (1994) two each from France, Germany, Italy, Spain and the UK; one each from the other member countries apart from Luxembourg. Headquarters in Brussels. The European Commission can be referred to as **Brussels** in headlines, etc.

European Court of Human Rights
The court, which sits in Strasbourg, was set up by the 21 members of the Council of Europe; it tries to ensure the observance of the European Convention on Human Rights. Its decisions are not binding on British courts.

European Court of Justice
The court safeguards the law in the interpretation and application of EU treaties. Most of its cases are business related. Its decisions are binding on British courts. Headquarters is in Luxembourg.

European Free Trade Association (Efta)

Efta was set up to promote free trade in industrial goods among its members, later to create a single market in western Europe. Agreement was reached on a **European Economic Area (EEA)** composed of all Efta and EC countries in 1992, but after the Swiss rejected the agreement it was signed by the other Efta countries and the EC Commission in 1993. Efta members are Austria, Finland, Iceland, Liechtenstein, Norway, Sweden and Switzerland. It is based in Geneva.

European Investment Bank (EIB)

The EIB finances capital investment within and outside the EU. Headquarters in Luxembourg.

European Parliament

The European Parliament meets in Strasbourg or Brussels. Until June 1994 it had 518 seats: France, Germany, Italy, UK 81 each; Spain 60; Netherlands 25; Belgium, Greece, Portugal 24; Denmark 16; Ireland 15; Luxembourg 6. After the June 1994 elections the parliament expanded to 567 seats: Germany 99, UK, France, Italy 87, Spain 64, Netherlands 31, Belguim, Greece, Portugal 25, Denmark 16, Ireland 15, Luxembourg 6. Headquarters is in Luxembourg; committees meet in Brussels.

European Space Agency (ESA)

The ESA promotes space research and technology and implementation of European space policy. Based in Paris.

European Union (EU), formerly European Community (EC)

Part of the European Communities, which include the European Coal and Steel Community and European Atomic Energy Community (Euratom). EC members are: Belgium, France, Germany, Italy, Luxembourg, Netherlands (founder signatories Treaty of Rome 1951; founder members EEC 1957), UK, Denmark, Ireland (joined 1973), Greece (joined 1981), Portugal, Spain (joined 1986). Turkey applied for membership in 1987. Further enlargement is likely. EC headquarters is in Brussels.

Federal Reserve Board (Fed)

Consists of 12 regional Federal Reserve Banks in the US and a board of governors of the Federal Reserve System. The US central banking system.

Francophonie
The French-speaking equivalent of the Commonwealth, set up in 1986; 38 countries are members.

General Agreement on Tariffs and Trade (Gatt)
A UN specialised agency based in Geneva responsible for the only internationally accepted trade treaty; 110 states are contracting parties with another 23 countries applying Gatt rules on a de facto basis.

Group of Five (G5)
A subset of the **Group of Ten**, it consists of the finance ministers and central bank governors of Britain, France, Germany, the US and Japan. It holds occasional meetings.

Group of Seven (G7)
G7 consists of the world's largest industrial democracies: the US, Japan, Germany, Britain, France, Italy, Canada. Government leaders hold annual summits.

Group of Ten
A group of leading industrial countries originally institutionalised to provide funds for the IMF. It includes Switzerland so membership is actually 11.

Members are: UK, US, Germany, France, Italy, the Netherlands, Belgium, Sweden, Canada, Japan and Switzerland.

Group of 24 (G24)

A group of industrialised nations set up to provide financial support for the countries of eastern Europe. It consists of the member states of the **OECD**, *qv*.

The same name is also used by a group of developing countries set up to represent their interests in the international financial community. Its members are Algeria, Argentina, Brazil, Colombia, Côte d'Ivoire, Egypt, Ethiopia, Gabon, Ghana, Guatemala, India, Iran, Lebanon, Mexico, Nigeria, Pakistan, Peru, Philippines, Sri Lanka, Syria, Trinidad and Tobago, Venezuela, Yugoslavia and Zaire.

Group of 77 (G77)

A grouping of developing countries which was set up with 77 members but now includes more than 120 countries.

Gulf Co-operation Council (GCC)

Members are Bahrain, Kuwait, Oman, Qatar, Saudi Arabia and the United Arab Emirates.

International Atomic Energy Agency (IAEA)

A UN body based in Vienna which aims to promote the uses of atomic energy for peaceful purposes. It has 114 member states.

International Air Transport Association (Iata)

An association in which airlines negotiate fare structures. Headquarters in Montreal and Geneva.

International Confederation of Free Trade Unions

Aims to promote free trade unionism worldwide. 164 unions in 117 countries are affiliated. Headquarters in Brussels.

International Court of Justice

A United Nations body which sits in The Hague; its objective is the peaceful settlement of disputes between states, usually but not necessarily members of the UN. Also known as the **World Court**.

International Energy Agency (IEA)
An autonomous agency within the OECD founded after the 1973 oil crisis, it aims to improve energy supply and demand worldwide and to develop alternative energy sources. Based in Paris.

International Maritime Satellite Organisation (Inmarsat)
Operates a system of satellites to provide telephone, telex, data and facsimile transmission services to the world's shipping, aviation and offshore industries. Based in London.

International Monetary Fund (IMF)
A UN body promoting international monetary co-operation, the expansion of international trade and exchange rate stability. It is based in Washington, DC.

International Red Cross and Red Crescent Movement
The movement consists of (a) the International Committee of the Red Cross (ICRC), a neutral intermediary between warring factions which tries to ensure application of the Geneva Conventions; (b) the International Federation of Red Cross and Red Crescent Societies, which aims to co-ordinate relief work and care for refugees outside areas of conflict (societies exist in 150 countries); and (c) the International Conference of the Red Cross and Red Crescent, which meets every four years, bringing together representatives from these bodies and national societies. The movement is based in Geneva.

International Standards Organisation (ISO)
A forum of standards bodies from around 80 nations. A non-treaty body of the UN.

International Telecommunications Satellite Organisation (Intelsat)
Intelsat owns and operates the worldwide commercial telecommunications satellite system. It provides international telephone and television services. Headquarters in Washington, DC.

Interpol (International Criminal Police Organisation)
Promotes co-operation between criminal police authorities. Based in Lyons, France. Interpol is acceptable at all references.

League of Arab States
The league aims to ensure co-operation among its members and protect their independence. It has 21 members. Headquarters in Cairo, Egypt.

Médecins sans Frontières
Paris-based medical charity group which operates in countries suffering from famine or war.

Mercosur
A free trade zone set up in 1990 as the result of a treaty signed by Argentina, Brazil, Paraguay and Uruguay. It is intended to come into full operation in 1995. Preferred spelling is the Spanish **Mercosur**, rather than the Portuguese **Mercosul**.

Nato (North Atlantic Treaty Organisation)
It is acceptable to write just Nato at all references. Members of Nato are: Belgium, Canada, Denmark, France, Germany, Greece, Iceland, Italy, Luxembourg, Netherlands, Norway, Portugal, Spain, Turkey, UK, US. France and Iceland do not belong to the military committee. Headquarters in Brussels.

Organisation of African Unity (OAU)
A cultural, political, scientific and economic grouping of black African states; 51 members. Headquarters in Addis Ababa, Ethiopia.

Organisation of American States (OAS)
Members are 35 countries in North, Central and South America. Headquarters in Washington, DC.

Organisation of Arab Petroleum Exporting Countries (Oapec)
Members are: Algeria, Bahrain, Egypt, Iraq, Kuwait, Libya, Qatar, Saudi Arabia, Syria, UAE. Tunisia's membership is inactive. Headquarters in Cairo, Egypt.

Organisation for Economic Co-operation and Development (OECD)
A group of countries whose aim is to promote stable economic growth and welfare. Members are: Australia, Austria, Belgium, Canada, Denmark, Finland, France, Germany, Greece, Iceland, Ireland, Italy, Japan, Luxembourg, Netherlands, New Zealand, Norway, Portugal, Spain, Sweden, Switzerland, Turkey, UK, US. Headquarters in Paris.

Organisation of the Islamic Conference (OIC)
The OIC was formed in 1971 with the aim of generating co-operation among Islamic countries. Its heads of state meet every three years, its foreign ministers annually. The OIC has 51 member (49 states plus the Palestine Liberation Organisation and Zanzibar). Headquarters in Jeddah, Saudi Arabia.

Organisation of Petroleum Exporting Countries (Opec)
Members are: Algeria, Ecuador, Gabon, Indonesia, Iran, Iraq, Kuwait, Libya, Nigeria, Qatar, Saudi Arabia, UAE, Venezuela. Based in Vienna.

Paris Club
A group of industrial countries meeting regularly in Paris to discuss debt rescheduling of debtor countries with payments difficulties.

Privy Council
The private council of the British sovereign, consisting of all present and former ministers and other distinguished individuals, all of whom are appointed for life. The judicial committee of the Privy Council is the highest court of appeal for some Commonwealth countries.

Supreme Headquarters Allied Powers Europe (Shape)
Nato's military headquarters, based in Mons, Belgium.

UNITED NATIONS
Founded in 1945 with 50 signatories, the UN currently has 184 member states. It is based in New York.

UN is acceptable in all references to the United Nations; stories should be datelined from New York or Geneva, not from the UN.

The principal organs of the UN are:

The General Assembly. All members belong and have five representatives and one vote each. Its seven main committees deal with security, financial, social, decolonisation, administrative, legal and political matters.

The Economic and Social Council has 54 members elected for a three-year term. It is responsible for co-ordinating the work of the specialised UN agencies and other UN bodies.

International Court of Justice consists of 15 judges each elected for a nine-year term. Based in The Hague, its objective is the peaceful settlement of disputes between states, usually but not necessarily members of the UN.

The Secretariat is headed by the UN secretary-general, who is elected by a majority vote of the General Assembly.

The Security Council consists of 15 members, five permanent and 10 elected for a two-year term. It bears primary responsibility for the maintenance of peace and security.

The Trusteeship Council supervises the administration of territories within the UN Trusteeship system. Only the Republic of Palau remains within the system.

OTHER UN BODIES
Conference on Disarmament Geneva, Switzerland
Office of the UN Disaster and Relief Co-ordinator (Undro)
 Geneva
UN Centre for Human Settlements (Habitat) Nairobi, Kenya
UN Children's Fund (Unicef) New York
UN Commission for Trade and Development (Unctad) Geneva
UN Development Programme (UNDP) New York
UN Environment Programme (Unep) Nairobi
UN Fund for Population Activities (UNFPA) New York
UN High Commissioner for Refugees (UNHCR) Geneva
UN Institute for the Advancement of Women (Instraw) Santo Domingo,
 Dominican Republic
UN Institute for Training and Research (Unitar) New York
**UN Relief and Works Agency for Palestine Refugees in the Near
 East (UNRWA)** Vienna
UN Sudano-Sahelian Office (UNSO)
UN University (UNU) Tokyo
World Food Council (WFC) Rome
World Food Programme (WFP) Rome

SPECIALISED AGENCIES OF THE UN
Food and Agriculture Organisation (FAO) Rome
International Bank for Reconstruction and Development (IBRD)
 Washington DC (this is the **World Bank**, *qv*)
International Civil Aviation Organisation (ICAO) Montreal,
 Canada
International Development Agency (IDA) Washington, DC
International Finance Corporation (IDC) Washington, DC
International Fund for Agricultural Development (Ifad) Rome
International Labour Organisation (ILO) *Geneva*

International Maritime Organisation (IMO) London
International Monetary Fund (IMF) *qv* Washington DC
International Telecommunications Union (ITU) Geneva
United Nations Educational, Scientific and Cultural Organisation (Unesco) Paris
United Nations Industrial Development Organisation (Unido) Vienna.
Universal Postal Union (UPU) Berne, Switzerland
World Health Organisation (WHO) Geneva
World Intellectual Property Organisation (Wipo) Geneva
World Meteorological Organisation (WMO) Geneva
World Tourism Organisation Madrid, Spain

RELATED ORGANISATIONS
International Atomic Energy Agency (IAEA) Vienna
General Agreement on Tariffs and Trade (Gatt) Geneva

Western European Union (WEU)
Provides self-defence, economic, cultural and social collaboration among its members. The WEU consists of the EU countries except Denmark and Ireland, which have observer status only. Iceland, Norway and Turkey are associate members.

The Maastricht treaty of 1993 proposed placing EU defence responsibilities in the hands of the WEU. The WEU's assembly meets twice a year in Paris. Headquarters is in Brussels.

World Bank
Full title is the International Bank for Reconstruction and Development; second and later references: **the bank**. The World Bank is a UN agency financing development in non-industrialised countries. **The International Development Agency (IDA)** and **International Finance Corporation (IDC)** are affiliated. The World Bank is based in Washington, DC.

World Council of Churches (WCC)
Promotes unity among Christian churches. It has 322 member churches from over 100 countries. Based in Geneva.

World Court see **International Court of Justice.**

SHIPPING GLOSSARY

Baltic Exchange City of London market which matches cargoes and ships or aircraft. It also deals in commodity futures.

barratry vexatious litigation; in marine law, fraud or negligence by the master or crew, to the owner's disadvantage.

charterparty a contract under which a charterer has the use of a ship for a specified voyage or a certain time.

cif (cost insurance and freight) a cif price includes all the charges paid by an exporter up to the port of delivery. *See* **fob**.

deadweight weight that a vessel is capable of carrying when loaded to the maximum permitted marks. It is measured in long tons (2,240lb) or tonnes (2,204lb). A ship is referred to as, eg, **100,000dwt**.

fob (free on board) a price is free on board when a seller delivers goods to a ship or lorry at his own cost with the understanding that the buyer pays transport and other subsequent charges. *See* **cif**.

gross registered tonnage (grt) total enclosed capacity in a ship, minus certain exempted spaces.

knot one nautical mile per hour; a nautical mile is 6,080ft.

Lloyd's Register of Shipping an annually produced list of vessels of more than 100 tons classified according to seaworthiness. It has no direct connection with Lloyd's of London insurance market. **A1 at Lloyd's** is the top classification for ships.

manifest list of cargo carried on a ship or aircraft.

ro-ro roll on-roll off ferry; ro-ro at second reference.

a ship is **it** not **she**; people serve **in** it, not on it; a **boat** is a small open craft or a submarine.

212

teu (twenty foot equivalent units) a measure of the area of a ship; eg, **100teu**.

ULCC an ultra large crude carrier is generally taken to mean a tanker of 320,000dwt or more.

VLCC a very large crude carrier is regarded as a carrier of not less than 160,000dwt.

STATES, PROVINCES, COUNTIES AND REGIONS

AUSTRALIA

States and territories
Australian Capital Territory, New South Wales, Northern Territory, Queensland, South Australia, Tasmania, Victoria, Western Australia.

BELGIUM

Provinces
Antwerp, Brabant, East Flanders, Hainaut, Liège, Limbourg, Luxembourg, Namur, West Flanders.

BRITAIN

Great Britain is England, Scotland and Wales; it is sufficient to write **Britain**; the **UK** is England, Scotland, Wales and Northern Ireland; the **British Isles** is the whole lot including Ireland. The Isle of Man and the Channel Islands are crown dependencies; they are part of the British Isles but not part of the UK.

CANADA

Provinces
Alberta, British Columbia, Manitoba, New Brunswick, Newfoundland and Labrador, Nova Scotia, Ontario, Prince Edward Island, Quebec, Saskatchewan.

Territories
Northwest Territories, Yukon Territory.

Atlantic Provinces
New Brunswick, Nova Scotia, Prince Edward Island, Newfoundland.

Maritime Provinces
New Brunswick, Nova Scotia, Prince Edward Island.

COMMONWEALTH OF INDEPENDENT STATES
A grouping of states which were formerly constituent republics of the Soviet Union.

214

Population and capital in parentheses
Armenia (3.3m, Yerevan)
Belarus (10.1m, Minsk)
Kazakhstan (16.5m, Alma-Ata)
Kyrgyzstan (4.3m, Bishkek)
Moldova (4.3m, Kishinev)
Russia/Russian Federation (148m, Moscow)
Tajikistan (5.1m, Dushanbe)
Turkmenistan (3.5m, Ashkhabad)
Ukraine (51.5m, Kiev)
Uzbekistan (19.8m, Tashkent).

Georgia (5.4m, Tbilisi) is a former Soviet republic but has not joined the CIS. Azerbaijan (7m, Baku) refused to ratify CIS membership because of Russian support for Armenia in the war over Nagorno-Karabakh.

Armenia, Azerbaijan, Belarus, Georgia, Moldova, Russia and Ukraine are covered on the European news pages of the FT.

Kazakhstan, Kyrgyzstan, Tajikistan, Turkmenistan and Uzbekistan are covered on the International news pages.

ENGLAND

Counties
Avon, Bedfordshire, Berkshire, Buckinghamshire, Cambridgeshire, Cheshire, Cleveland, Cornwall, Cumbria, Derbyshire, Devon, Dorset, Durham, East Sussex, Essex, Gloucestershire, Hampshire, Hereford and Worcester, Hertfordshire, Humberside, Isle of Wight, Kent, Lancashire, Leicestershire, Lincolnshire, Norfolk, Northamptonshire, Northumberland, North Yorkshire, Nottinghamshire, Oxfordshire, Shropshire, Somerset, Staffordshire, Suffolk, Surrey, Warwickshire, West Sussex, Wiltshire.

Metropolitan counties
Greater Manchester, Merseyside, South Yorkshire, Tyne and Wear, West Midlands, West Yorkshire.

FAR EAST
Usually China, Hong Kong, Japan, Macao, Mongolia, Taiwan. But avoid the term if possible because these countries are neither far from, nor east of, many FT readers. Prefer **East Asia**.

FRANCE

Regions
Alsace, Aquitaine, Auvergne, Burgundy (Bourgogne), Brittany (Bretagne), Centre, Champagne-Ardenne, Corsica (Corse), Franche-Comté, Ile-de-France, Languedoc-Roussillon, Limousin, Lorraine, Midi-Pyrénées, Nord-Pas-de-Calais, Basse-Normandie, Haute-Normandie, Pays de la Loire, Picardy (Picardie), Poitou-Charentes, Provence-Alpes-Côte d'Azur, Rhône-Alpes.

FT style is the unbracketed spelling.

GERMANY

Former West German states (Länder)
Baden-Württemberg, Bavaria (Bayern), Berlin, Bremen, Hamburg, Hesse (Hessen), Lower Saxony (Niedersachsen), North-Rhine Westphalia (Nord-Rhein Westfalen), Rhineland-Palatinate (Rheinland-Pfalz), Saarland, Schleswig-Holstein.

Former East German states
Brandenburg, Mecklenburg, Sachsen (Saxony), Sachsen-Anhalt, Thuringia.

FT style is the unbracketed spelling.

INDIA

States
Andhra Pradesh, Arunachal Pradesh, Assam, Bihar, Goa, Gujarat, Haryana, Himachal Pradesh, Jammu and Kashmir (disputed), Karnataka, Kerala, Madhya Pradesh, Maharashtra, Manipur, Meghalaya, Mizoram, Nagaland, Orissa, Punjab, Rajasthan, Sikkim, Tamil Nadu, Tripura, Uttar Pradesh, West Bengal.

Union territories
Andaman and Nicobar Is., Chandigarh, Dadra and Nagar Haveli, Daman and Diu, Delhi, Lakshadweep, Pondicherry.

INDIAN SUBCONTINENT
Bangladesh, Bhutan, India, Nepal, Pakistan, Sikkim and Sri Lanka.

INDOCHINA consists of the countries of the south-east Asian peninsula: Burma, Cambodia, Laos, Malaysia, Thailand, Vietnam.

IRELAND
The southern part is the **Republic of Ireland** or the **Irish Republic**, never Eire (which is the Irish word for Ireland).

Provinces (counties in parentheses)
Connacht (Galway, Leitrim, Mayo, Roscommon, Sligo).

Leinster (Carlow, Dublin, Kildare, Kilkenny, Laoighis, Longford, Louth, Meath, Offaly, Westmeath, Wexford, Wicklow).

Munster (Clare, Cork, Kerry, Limerick, Tipperary North Riding, Tipperary South Riding, Waterford).

Ulster (Cavan, Donegal, Monaghan).

ITALY

Regions
Abruzzi, Basilicata, Calabria, Campania, Emilia Romagna, Friuli-Venezia Giulia, Lazio, Liguria, Lombardy (Lombardia), Marche, Molise, Piedmont (Piemonte), Puglia, Sardinia (Sardegna), Sicily (Sicilia), Tuscany (Toscana), Trentino-Alto Adige, Umbria, Valle d'Aosta, Veneto.

FT style is the unbracketed spelling.

MAGHREB
The countries of north-west Africa: Algeria, Libya, Mauritania, Morocco, Tunisia, Western Sahara.

MIDDLE EAST
Bahrain, Cyprus, Egypt, Iran, Iraq, Israel, Jordan, Kuwait, Lebanon, Oman, Qatar, Saudi Arabia, Sudan, Syria, Turkey, United Arab Emirates, Yemen.

Do not write Near East. **Mideast** is acceptable in single column headlines.

NETHERLANDS

Provinces
Drenthe, Flevoland, Friesland, Gelderland, Groningen, Limburg, Noord-Brabant, Noord-Holland, Overijssel, Utrecht, Zeeland, Zuid-Holland.

NEW ENGLAND consists of Connecticut, Maine, Massachusetts, New Hampshire, Rhode Island and Vermont.

NORDIC COUNTRIES
Denmark, Finland, Iceland, Norway and Sweden.

NORTHERN IRELAND

Ulster or **the province** can be used as variants of Northern Ireland.

Counties
Antrim, Armagh, Down, Fermanagh, Londonderry, Tyrone.

SAHEL is the southern border of the Sahara desert; 22 countries are in the Sahel region, which is prone to drought, and are members of **Club du Sahel**, a multilateral donor organisation. The UN Sudano-Sahelian Office (Unso) co-ordinates relief efforts.

SCANDINAVIA
Denmark, Norway and Sweden.

SCOTLAND

Regions
Borders, Central, Dumfries and Galloway, Fife, Grampian, Highland, Lothian, Orkney, Shetland, Strathclyde, Tayside, Western Isles.
Note: Grampian, Highland and Strathclyde are very large and a lot of Central is not particularly central. Therefore refer to the county name instead: **Oban, Argyll**, rather than **Oban, Strathclyde**. In the International Edition **Oban, Scotland** is acceptable. Cities can also be used as locators: **Paisley near Glasgow**.

SOUTH AFRICAN "HOMELANDS"
Areas of South Africa which were set aside for occupation by the black population: Gazankulu, Lebowa, KwaNdbele, KaNgwane, Qwaqwa and KwaZulu were designated self-governing national states. Four others, Bophuthatswana, Ciskei, Transkei and Venda were regarded as independent republics by the South African government but were not recognised by the UN.

SOVIET UNION *see* **Commonwealth of Independent States**

UNITED ARAB EMIRATES
Consists of Abu Dhabi, Dubai, Sharjah, Fujeirah, Ras al Khaimah, Ajman and Umm al Quwain.

UNITED KINGDOM

The **United Kingdom** consists of England, Wales, Scotland and Northern Ireland; **Great Britain** is England, Wales and Scotland only: write **Britain; the British Isles** is the whole lot including the Republic of Ireland.

UNITED STATES OF AMERICA

States

Alabama, Alaska, Arizona, Arkansas, California, Colorado, Connecticut, Delaware, Florida, Georgia, Hawaii, Idaho, Illinois, Indiana, Iowa, Kansas, Kentucky, Louisiana, Maine, Maryland, Massachusetts, Michigan, Minnesota, Mississippi, Missouri, Montana, Nebraska, Nevada, New Hampshire, New Jersey, New Mexico, New York, North Carolina, North Dakota, Ohio, Oklahoma, Oregon, Pennsylvania, Rhode Island, South Carolina, South Dakota, Tennessee, Texas, Utah, Vermont, Virginia, Washington, West Virginia, Wisconsin, Wyoming.

WALES

Counties

Clwyd, Dyfed, Gwent, Gwynedd, Mid Glamorgan, Powys, South Glamorgan, West Glamorgan.

The eight Welsh counties and 37 districts are due to be replaced by 21 unitary authorities by 1995. Clwyd, Dyfed, Gwent, Gwynedd and Powys will disappear, and Monmouthshire, Pembrokeshire, Carmarthenshire, Cardiganshire, etc, will reappear along with new districts.

YUGOSLAVIA

Yugoslavia was a federation consisting of six republics (population and capitals in parentheses):

Bosnia-Hercegovina (4.1m, Sarajevo)
Croatia (4.7m, Zagreb)
Macedonia (1.9m, Skopje)
Montenegro (650,000, Podgorica)
Serbia (9.3m, Belgrade)
Slovenia (1.8m, Ljubljana)

As this book goes to press Slovenia and Croatia are independent republics; Macedonia's independence has not been internationally recognised because of Greek objections to its name (Macedonia is also a Greek province); Serbia (which includes the provinces of Kosovo and Vojvodina) and Montenegro remain part of the rump federation of Yugoslavia, not recognised internationally because of Serbian aggression in Bosnia; and Bosnia-Hercegovina, recognised as an independent state by the EU and the US, and a member of the UN, is in the middle of a civil war between its Serb, Moslem and Croat communities.

STOCK MARKET INDICES

The UK's first stock market index was the Financial Times Index first published (by the Financial News, which the FT later absorbed) in 1935. It was known as the Thirty-Share Index, and is sometimes still known as this. It was renamed the **Financial Times Ordinary Share Index** in 1984.

This index was not a good long-term measure of portfolio performance. In 1962 the FT therefore introduced the **FT-Actuaries All-Share Index** to remedy the defect. This is the most broadly based index, with more than 800 constituent shares.

The **Financial Times-Stock Exchange (FT-SE) 100 Share Index** was introduced in 1984 to fill the need for a constantly updated index – the FT Index at the time was updated only once an hour. The FT-SE is generally known as **Footsie** and is based on the price of 100 leading shares. It is the key indicator of the market's mood and is calculated once a minute during trading hours.

In 1992, the FT, the London Stock Exchange and the actuarial profession brought most of their indices together into the FT-SE Actuaries series of indices, launching several more indices in the process.

The closing values of several indices appear on the front page of the FT each day in the Markets table, and in more detail on the relevant statistics pages. Details of all the FT indices are given below.

FT INDICES

1. FT-SE Actuaries Share Indices: The UK Series

In association with the London Stock Exchange and the UK actuarial profession (the Institute of Actuaries in England and the Faculty of Actuaries in Scotland). These indices differ in their coverage, but all are calculated according to a common set of published ground rules.

FT-SE 100 Index (FT-SE). Calculated once a minute from 08.30 to 16.30. It covers the 100 largest companies by market capitalisation. Changes to constituents are made once a quarter, according to a narrowly defined formula. Close, recent days and historic highs and lows, as well as hourly changes are shown on the London Stock Exchange page. On first reference try to refer to this index as the **FT-SE 100,** to distinguish it from other recently introduced FT-SE indices.

FT-SE Mid-250. The 250 companies ranking just below the FT-SE 100 in market capitalisation. It was introduced in autumn 1992, but a back-calculation exists to 1984 or so. These mid-sized companies are more directly exposed to the vagaries of the UK economy than the larger, international blue chips in the FT-SE 100. The performance of the two indices may thus vary widely in the short run.

FT-SE Actuaries 350. The FT-SE 100 plus the FT-SE Mid 250. This may in time become an important benchmark of the more liquid stocks. For the moment, however, it is principally useful because it is used as the basis for calculating **FT-SE Actuaries 350 Industry Baskets**, which are real-time indices modelled on the FT-A All-Share sectors. They allow investors to keep an eye on how individual industry sectors are doing during the day. The definitive end-of-day record of sectoral performance remains the FT-A All-Share.

FT-SE Actuaries All-Share. Calculated once a day. This series of indices is shown daily on the page that carries the London Stock Market report. This index is elaborately subdivided; its components ought to be correctly distinguished from each other:

> **FT-SE Actuaries All-Share (All-Share)**. Currently around 850 companies.

> **Non-Financials**. This category, which contains 631 companies, is the successor to the old FT-Actuaries 500 index. It has traditionally been used by analysts to calculate price/earnings ratios for the market as a whole. Since the reclassification of January 1994, Non-Financials are divided into five main industry groups: **Mineral Extraction**, **General Manufactures**, **Consumer Goods**, **Services** and **Utilities**. **Financials** and **Investment Trusts** complete the All-Share. Each of these broad groups is divided into many individual sectors (Engineering, Pharmaceuticals, Media, Banks, etc).

> **FT-SE SmallCap** contains those FT-A All-Share constituents which are too small to qualify for the FT-SE 350. This index and the Mid-250 are calculated with and without investment trusts.

2. FT-SE Actuaries Share Indices: The European Series

In association with the London Stock Exchange and the UK actuarial profession (the Institute of Actuaries in England and the Faculty of Actuaries in Scotland).

FT-SE Eurotrack 100 Index (FT-SE Eurotrack) and FT-SE Eurotrack 200 Index. Calculated once a minute from 09.45 to 15.30. The 100 index contains

Continental stocks; the 200 contains those in the 100 plus the top UK stocks measured by the FT-SE 100. The relative weighting of each country's shares reflects its market capitalisation. Close, recent days and historic highs and lows as well as hourly changes are shown on the World Stock Markets page.

3. FT-Actuaries Fixed Interest Indices

In association with the UK actuarial profession (the Institute of Actuaries in England and the Faculty of Actuaries in Scotland).

Calculated once a day. These cover UK government bonds (gilts) and other UK fixed interest stocks. **The FT-Actuaries All Fixed Interest Stocks Index** covers all fixed maturity and irredeemable gilts; there is a similar index for index linked gilts.

4. FT-Actuaries World Indices (FT-AWI)

In association with the UK actuarial profession (the Institute of Actuaries in England and the Faculty of Actuaries in Scotland, and with the investment banks Goldman Sachs and NatWest Markets).

Calculated once a day. This series of indices is shown daily in the table of the same name that normally appears on the second World Stock Markets page. The indices are published in US dollars, sterling, yen and D-Marks for the world, 11 regions and 24 constituent countries.

Note: for legal reasons, attribution to The Financial Times Ltd, Goldman Sachs & Co. and NatWest Securities Ltd *must* be made on tables and charts. It is not required in normal text references.

5. Other indices that the FT calculates

Financial Times Ordinary Share Index (FT Index). Thirty constituents – calculated once a minute from 08.30 to 16.30. Close, recent days and historic highs and lows, as well as hourly changes are shown on London Stock Exchange page. The constituent companies change from time to time.

FT Government Securities Index. Calculated once a day. Close, recent days and historic highs and lows are shown on the London Stock Exchange page.

FT Fixed Interest Index. Calculated once a day. Recently revised to include all large publicly quoted gold mining companies worldwide. Close, recent days and historic highs and lows are shown on the World Stock Markets page.

FT Gold Mines Index. Calculated once a day. Close, recent days and historic highs and lows are shown on the London Stock Exchange page.

FT Index of Gilt-Edged Bargains. Calculated once a day. Close and previous day's close are shown on the London Stock Exchange page.

OTHER UK INDICES

A long-running small-company index, the **Hoare Govett Small Company Index** is published in the Weekend FT Finance and the Family pages.

OVERSEAS INDICES

In the US the principal indicator is the **Dow Jones Industrial Average** (though many stock market professionals use the **Standard & Poor's 500**, also referred to as the **S&P Composite**). In Germany it is the **DAX index**; in Paris the **CAC-40** index; in Italy the **MIB General** index; in Stockholm the **Affärsvärlden** index; in Tokyo the **Nikkei**; in Australia the **All Ordinaries** index; in Hong Kong the **Hang Seng** index.

These and others are listed on the World Stock Markets page.

Two emerging markets indices are published in the FT weekly. That calculated by the World Bank's IFC affiliate is published on Thursdays; that calculated by the Barings merchant bank on Mondays.

TRADE UNIONS

Only occasionally is it necessary to spell out the full name of a trade union that is normally referred to by its initials. Instead, a descriptive phrase is used as listed below.

The Amalgamated Engineering and Electrical Union and its EEPTU electrical wing or AEU engineering wing

Aslef, the train drivers' union

The Apex white collar section of the GMB general union

Balpa, the airline pilots' union

Bifu, the banking and insurance union

Cohse, the health service union

The CPSA civil service union

The EEPTU electricians' union

Equity, the actors' union

The FDA senior civil servants' union

The Fire Brigades Union

The GMB general union

The Institute of Journalists

The IPMS specialists' civil service union or the IPMS, which represents specialist and managerial civil servants

The Inland Revenue Staff Federation

The ISTC steel union

The MSF general technical union or the white collar union MSF

The Musicians' Union

The public service union Nalgo

The Nacods pit supervisors' union or pit deputies' union

The NAS/UWT teachers' union

The NCU communications union

The NUCPS civil service union

The National Union of Journalists

The National Union of Mineworkers

The Nupe public service union

The National Union of Teachers

The Prison Officers' Association

RMT, the rail workers' and seamen's union

Sogat, the print union

The TGWU general union or the TGWU public service union

TSSA, the white collar rail union

The UCW postal workers' union

Ucatt, the construction union

Unison, the public service union

Usdaw, the shopworkers' union

REFERENCE BOOKS

Accountancy
The Economist Pocket Accountant by Christopher Nobes. Basil Blackwell and The Economist.

Air
Jane's All the World's Aircraft. Jane's Information Group.
Flight International Directory.

Arts
New Grove Dictionary of Music and Musicians. Macmillan.
Who's Who in the Theatre. Gale Research, Detroit.

Companies
City Code on Takeovers and Mergers. The Panel on Takeovers and Mergers.
Crawford's Directory of City Connections. The Economist Directories.
Directory of Directors. Reed Information Services.
Hambro Company Guide
Stock Exchange Year Book. London Stock Exchange.
Who owns Whom

Financial Statistics
A Guide to Financial Times Statistics
Economic Trends and Financial Statistics, published monthly by the Central Statistical Office
Monthly Digest of Statistics. Central Statistical Office
Bank of England Bulletin (quarterly)
Employment Gazette (monthly)
International Financial Statistics (International Monetary Fund, monthly)
Forecasts and trends are published at regular intervals by the Confederation of British Industry, the Treasury, the National Insititue of Economic and Social Research, the London Business School and other bodies. International economic statistics are published by the Organisation for Economic Co-operation and Development (OECD).

International affairs
The Statesman's Year-book. Macmillan Reference Books.
Whitaker's Almanac.

International companies
Asian Company Handbook Toyo Keizai.
Japan Company Handbook Toyo Keizai.
Standard & Poor's Stock Guide for US companies.

Language
Most of these books are updated regularly
Brewer's Dictionary of Phrase and Fable. Cassell.
The Complete Plain Words by Sir Ernest Gowers. Penguin Books
The Concise Oxford Dictionary. Clarendon Press, Oxford.
Collins English Dictionary. Harper Collins.
Fowler's Modern English Usage by H.W. Fowler. Oxford University Press
Hart's Rules for Compositors and Readers. Oxford University Press.
The New Collins Thesaurus. Harper Collins.
The Oxford Dictionary of Modern Quotations. Oxford University Press.
The Oxford Book of Quotations. Oxford University Press.
The Oxford Dictionary for Writers and Editors. Clarendon Press, Oxford.
The New Penguin Dictionary of Quotations. Viking
Penguin Spelling Dictionary. Penguin Books
Roget's Thesaurus. Longman Dictionaries.
Waterhouse on Newspaper Style. Viking.
A Word in Time by Philip Howard. Sinclair Stevenson, 1990.

People
Who's Who. A & C Black.
International Who's Who. Europe International Publications.
Debrett's Peerage & Baronetage. Debrett's Peerage Ltd and Macmillan.
Who's Who in the City. London Stock Exchange.

Places
Kelly's Directories. Reed Information Services.
The Times Atlas of the World

Politicians
Vacher's Parliamentary Companion. Vacher's Publications.
Dod's Parliamentary Companion.

Shipping
Register of Ships. Lloyd's Register of Shipping
Jane's Fighting Ships. Jane's Information Group.

General

The Henderson Top 1,000 Charities. Henderson Administration Group.
Reuters Glossary: International Economic & Financial Terms
   Whitaker's Almanack contains much useful information.

Make sure you always have the latest edition of any reference book and remember that reference books quickly become out of date.

INDEX

The index is word-by word: stock split comes before stockholder. Short entries in the alphabetical section are not indexed. Abbreviations in the list on pages 139–148 are also not indexed. Glossary entries and subheadings in the reference section are indexed.